Editor
Mary S. Jones, M.A.

Editor in Chief
Karen J. Goldfluss, M.S. Ed.

Cover Artist
Diem Pascarella

Illustrator
Clint McKnight

Art Coordinator
Renée Mc Elwee

Imaging
The Development Source
James Edward Grace

Publisher

Mary D. Smith, M.S. Ed.

TCR 2556

Instant Math Practice

Standards-based exercises for year-round practice!

- Number and Operations
- Algebra
- Geometry
- Measurement and Data
- Problem Solving

Teacher Created Resources

Author
Damon James

Teacher Created Resources
6421 Industry Way
Westminster, CA 92683
www.teachercreated.com
ISBN: 978-1-4206-2556-1
© 2013 Teacher Created Resources
Made in U.S.A.

Teacher Created Resources

Table of Contents

Table of Contents

Introduction

The *Instant Math Practice* series was written to provide students with frequent opportunities to master and retain important math skills. The unit practice pages are designed to target and reinforce those skills. As students become active learners and discover important mathematical relationships, they are more likely to improve their problem-solving skills and gain a new-found confidence in math. When using this book, take every opportunity possible to incorporate the practice exercises into your current curriculum.

This book addresses a variety of math skills and topics that help students build foundational knowledge in the following areas: numbers and numeration, addition, subtraction, multiplication, division, fractions, decimals, money, geometric objects, length, capacity, data analysis, problem solving, and so much more. In addition, the multiple practice opportunities in each unit facilitate students' mastery of math skills and concepts.

How to Use the Activity Pages

There are over 120 student activity pages, with each page containing six practice sections. The contents of each practice page relate directly to the skills addressed on that page. However, each of the six sections is designed to allow students to practice a skill in different ways. For example, on a page that focuses on place value, students may be asked to represent an expanded number as a numeral, to write a numeral in a chart to show its place value, to express the value of a digit in the given numeral, or to show a number in word form. By offering a variety of ways to practice a math skill on any given page, students think about and learn multiple approaches to mastering that skill.

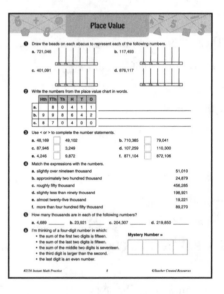

There are several ways in which to use the activities in this book. You may wish to coordinate each unit with whatever math concept is being introduced to the class. The student pages can be used to pre- or post-assess students as well. Practice pages can be assigned as homework or additional class work. An answer key is included in the back of the book.

Common Core State Standards Correlations (CCSS)

Each page of activities has been correlated to the Common Core State Standards for Math. For quick viewing of the math correlations, a chart is provided on pages 5 and 6 of this book. (Note: This version does not contain page titles but does reference the page numbers.) For a printable PDF version of the correlations chart, go to *www.teachercreated.com/standards/*. These charts correlate student page activities to applicable standards within a given domain.

Common Core State Standards Correlations

The student practice pages in *Instant Math Practice* meet one or more of the following Common Core State Standards © Copyright 2010. National Governors Association Center for Best Practices and Council of Chief State School Officers. All rights reserved. For more information about the Common Core State Standards, go to *http://www.corestandards.org/*.

Mathematics Standards	Page
Ratios & Proportional Relationships	
Understand ratio concepts and use ratio reasoning to solve problems.	
6.RP.1. Understand the concept of a ratio and use ratio language to describe a ratio relationship between two quantities.	69, 71, 72, 90
6.RP.2. Understand the concept of a unit rate a/b associated with a ratio a:b with b ≠ 0, and use rate language in the context of a ratio relationship.	73, 102
6.RP.3. Use ratio and rate reasoning to solve real-world and mathematical problems, e.g., by reasoning about tables of equivalent ratios, tape diagrams, double number line diagrams, or equations.	55, 56, 57, 58, 59, 60, 61, 71, 72, 127
The Number System	
Apply and extend previous understandings of multiplication and division to divide fractions by fractions.	
6.NS.1. Interpret and compute quotients of fractions, and solve word problems involving division of fractions by fractions, e.g., by using visual fraction models and equations to represent the problem.	41
Compute fluently with multi-digit numbers and find common factors and multiples.	
6.NS.2. Fluently divide multi-digit numbers using the standard algorithm.	21, 29, 30, 31, 32, 33, 34, 35, 36, 37, 66, 67, 68, 104, 122, 126
6.NS.3. Fluently add, subtract, multiply, and divide multi-digit decimals using the standard algorithm for each operation.	15, 20, 41, 42, 44, 45, 63, 64, 65, 66, 67, 68, 70, 97, 98, 99, 100, 101, 104, 122, 123, 124, 128
6.NS.4. Find the greatest common factor of two whole numbers less than or equal to 100 and the least common multiple of two whole numbers less than or equal to 12. Use the distributive property to express a sum of two whole numbers 1–100 with a common factor as a multiple of a sum of two whole numbers with no common factor.	25, 26, 27, 50
Apply and extend previous understandings of numbers to the system of rational numbers.	
6.NS.5. Understand that positive and negative numbers are used together to describe quantities having opposite directions or values (e.g., temperature above/below zero, elevation above/below sea level, credits/debits, positive/negative electric charge); use positive and negative numbers to represent quantities in real-world contexts, explaining the meaning of 0 in each situation.	51
6.NS.6. Understand a rational number as a point on the number line. Extend number line diagrams and coordinate axes familiar from previous grades to represent points on the line and in the plane with negative number coordinates.	51, 58, 62
6.NS.7. Understand ordering and absolute value of rational numbers.	56, 57, 62
6.NS.8. Solve real-world and mathematical problems by graphing points in all four quadrants of the coordinate plane. Include use of coordinates and absolute value to find distances between points with the same first coordinate or the same second coordinate.	95
Expressions & Equations	
Apply and extend previous understandings of arithmetic to algebraic expressions.	
6.EE.1. Write and evaluate numerical expressions involving whole-number exponents.	49
6.EE.2. Write, read, and evaluate expressions in which letters stand for numbers.	46, 47, 48
6.EE.3. Apply the properties of operations to generate equivalent expressions.	40

6.EE.4. Identify when two expressions are equivalent (i.e., when the two expressions name the same number regardless of which value is substituted into them).	39, 46, 47, 48, 122
Reason about and solve one-variable equations and inequalities.	
6.EE.5. Understand solving an equation or inequality as a process of answering a question: which values from a specified set, if any, make the equation or inequality true? Use substitution to determine whether a given number in a specified set makes an equation or inequality true.	29, 39, 44, 46, 47, 48
6.EE.6. Use variables to represent numbers and write expressions when solving a real-world or mathematical problem; understand that a variable can represent an unknown number, or, depending on the purpose at hand, any number in a specified set.	39, 44, 46, 47, 48
6.EE.7. Solve real-world and mathematical problems by writing and solving equations of the form $x + p = q$ and $px = q$ for cases in which p, q and x are all nonnegative rational numbers.	44, 45, 46, 47, 48
Represent and analyze quantitative relationships between dependent and independent variables.	
6.EE.9. Use variables to represent two quantities in a real-world problem that change in relationship to one another; write an equation to express one quantity, thought of as the dependent variable, in terms of the other quantity, thought of as the independent variable. Analyze the relationship between the dependent and independent variables using graphs and tables, and relate these to the equation. For example, in a problem involving motion at constant speed, list and graph ordered pairs of distances and times, and write the equation $d = 65t$ to represent the relationship between distance and time.	102, 118
Geometry	
Solve real-world and mathematical problems involving area, surface area, and volume.	
6.G.1. Find the area of right triangles, other triangles, special quadrilaterals, and polygons by composing into rectangles or decomposing into triangles and other shapes; apply these techniques in the context of solving real-world and mathematical problems.	106, 107
6.G.2. Find the volume of a right rectangular prism with fractional edge lengths by packing it with unit cubes of the appropriate unit fraction edge lengths, and show that the volume is the same as would be found by multiplying the edge lengths of the prism. Apply the formulas $V = l\,w\,h$ and $V = b\,h$ to find volumes of right rectangular prisms with fractional edge lengths in the context of solving real-world and mathematical problems.	109, 110
6.G.4. Represent three-dimensional figures using nets made up of rectangles and triangles, and use the nets to find the surface area of these figures. Apply these techniques in the context of solving real-world and mathematical problems.	86
Statistics & Probability	
Develop understanding of statistical variability.	
6.SP.1. Recognize a statistical question as one that anticipates variability in the data related to the question and accounts for it in the answers.	121
6.SP.2. Understand that a set of data collected to answer a statistical question has a distribution which can be described by its center, spread, and overall shape.	38, 116, 121
6.SP.3. Recognize that a measure of center for a numerical data set summarizes all of its values with a single number, while a measure of variation describes how its values vary with a single number.	38, 116
Summarize and describe distributions.	
6.SP.4. Display numerical data in plots on a number line, including dot plots, histograms, and box plots.	111, 113, 114, 115, 117, 118, 119, 121
6.SP.5. Summarize numerical data sets in relation to their context.	111, 112, 113, 114, 115, 117, 118, 119, 121

Numbers to One Million

❶ Write each of the following in numerals.

    a. five hundred twenty-one thousand, seven hundred two _____

    b. nine hundred thousand, five hundred seventy-six _____

    c. two hundred fifty thousand, eight hundred twenty _____

    d. six hundred eleven thousand, four hundred sixty-five _____

    e. one hundred eight thousand, two hundred thirty-nine _____

    f. ninety-five thousand, eight hundred ninety-one _____

❷ Write each of the numbers from question 1 as digits in the place value chart.

	Hth	TTh	Th	H	T	O
a.						
b.						
c.						
d.						
e.						
f.						

❸ Write the value of each of the underlined digits.

    a. 617,4<u>8</u>2 _____   **b.** 987,05<u>6</u> _____

    c. <u>7</u>32,517 _____   **d.** 46<u>8</u>,190 _____

    e. 8<u>7</u>5,215 _____   **f.** 104,<u>6</u>21 _____

❹ Complete each of the number series.

    a. 742,015; _____; _____; _____; 742,415

    b. 907,116; _____; _____; _____; 907,156

    c. 842,105; _____; _____; _____; 882,105

    d. 123,467; _____; _____; _____; 523,467

❺ Write the following numbers in words.

    a. 110,793 _____

    b. 248,916 _____

❻ Write the first eight numbers in a pattern, starting at one million and counting backwards by 2,000.

    ____1,000,000____; _____; _____; _____;

    _____; _____; _____; _____

Place Value

1 Draw the beads on each abacus to represent each of the following numbers.

a. 721,046

HTh	TTh	Th	H	T	O

b. 117,493

HTh	TTh	Th	H	T	O

c. 401,091

HTh	TTh	Th	H	T	O

d. 876,117

HTh	TTh	Th	H	T	O

2 Write the numbers from the place value chart in words.

	Hth	TTh	Th	H	T	O
a.		8	0	4	1	1
b.	9	9	8	6	4	2
c.	8	7	0	4	0	0

_____

_____

_____

3 Use < or > to complete the number statements.

a. 48,169 ☐ 49,102

b. 710,385 ☐ 79,041

c. 87,946 ☐ 3,249

d. 107,259 ☐ 110,300

e. 4,246 ☐ 9,872

f. 871,104 ☐ 872,106

4 Match the expressions with the numbers.

a. slightly over nineteen thousand   51,010

b. approximately two hundred thousand   24,879

c. roughly fifty thousand   456,285

d. slightly less than ninety thousand   198,921

e. almost twenty-five thousand   19,221

f. more than four hundred fifty thousand   89,270

5 How many thousands are in each of the following numbers?

a. 4,689 _____   **b.** 23,921 _____   **c.** 204,307 _____   **d.** 219,850 _____

6 I'm thinking of a four-digit number in which:
- the sum of the first two digits is fifteen.
- the sum of the last two digits is fifteen.
- the sum of the middle two digits is seventeen.
- the third digit is larger than the second.
- the last digit is an even number.

Mystery Number =

Numbers Greater than One Million

1 Write the value of the 5 in each of the following numbers.

    a. 1,072,315 _____

    c. 9,875,211 _____

    e. 1,115,216 _____

    b. 5,162,409 _____

    d. 4,573,429 _____

    f. 1,050,943 _____

2 Arrange each set of numbers in ascending order.

    a. 1,243,819; 1,346,721; 1,308,925 _____

    b. 2,487,905; 2,711,809; 2,635,921 _____

    c. 4,246,385; 4,105,907; 4,365,111 _____

3 Arrange each set of numbers in descending order.

    a. 8,051,987; 7,621,505; 7,921,300 _____

    b. 5,296,837; 5,121,352; 5,021,486 _____

    c. 7,932,481; 6,842,859; 8,110,425 _____

4 Round each number to the nearest million.

    a. 1,738,501 _____

    c. 992,106 _____

    e. 8,319,467 _____

    b. 6,219,850 _____

    d. 1,346,080 _____

    f. 4,511,909 _____

5 Write the place value of each of the underlined digits, then its value in the chart.

	Number	Place Value	Total Value
a.	39<u>8</u>,421		
b.	<u>8</u>,710,486		
c.	2,198,<u>7</u>04		
d.	3,94<u>7</u>,825		
e.	2<u>1</u>,843,211		
f.	4<u>2</u>7,806,921		

6 Is each of the following numbers closer to 50,000,000 or 60,000,000?

    a. 53,107,915 _____

    b. 54,681,999 _____

    c. 58,702,117 _____

Number Patterns

① Complete each of the following tables.

a.

1st No.	4	5	6	7	8
2nd No.	36	45	54		

b.

1st No.	26	36	46	56	66
2nd No.	45	55	65		

c.

1st No.	1.5	2.5	3.5	4.5	5.5
2nd No.	15	25	35		

d.

1st No.	46	56	66	76	86
2nd No.	38	48	58		

e.

1st No.	70	63	56	49	42
2nd No.		9			6

f.

1st No.	1	2	3	4	5
2nd No.	$\frac{1}{2}$				$2\frac{1}{2}$

② Write the rule for each of the number patterns in question 1 to show what you did to the 1st number to get the 2nd number.

a. _____ **b.** _____

c. _____ **d.** _____

e. _____ **f.** _____

③ Continue each of the following tricky number patterns.

a. 2, 3, 5, 8, _____, _____, _____   **b.** 2, 2.5, 3.5, 5, _____, _____, _____

c. 101, 82, 65, 50, _____, _____, _____   **d.** 2, 5, 11, 20, _____, _____, _____

④ Write a rule for each of the number patterns in question 3.

a. _____ **b.** _____

c. _____ **d.** _____

⑤ Look at the square numbers:

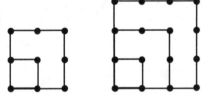

a. Write the rule to give the number of dots in each diagram. _____

b. What would be the 10th term in the pattern? _____

⑥ Apply the rule to complete the pattern: $2 \times \blacksquare + 5 = \blacktriangle$

■	2	4	6	8	10	12	14
▲							

Expanding Numbers

① Write the numeral for each of the following.

    a. 100,000 + 40,000 + 2,000 + 500 + 60 + 1 _____

    b. 600,000 + 8,000 + 90 + 6 _____

    c. 400,000 + 50,000 + 3,000 + 700 + 80 + 5 _____

    d. 800,000 + 70,000 + 800 + 7 _____

② Write each of the following in expanded notation.

    a. 56,409 _____

    b. 213,847 _____

    c. 462,001 _____

    d. 1,905,621 _____

③ How many tens are there in each of the following?

    a. 4,283 _____   **b.** 9,172 _____

    c. 48,632 _____   **d.** 27,485 _____

    e. 213,689 _____   **f.** 724,998 _____

④ How many thousands are there in each of the following?

    a. 4,639 _____   **b.** 21,486 _____

    c. 92,327 _____   **d.** 847,986 _____

    e. 123,428 _____   **f.** 1,428,376 _____

⑤ Use < or > to make the statements true.

    a. 4,320,146   ☐   4,000,000 + 300,000 + 20,000 + 1,000 + 400 + 60

    b. 100,000 + 40 + 6 + 200 + 7,000   ☐   170,246

⑥ True or false?

    a. 200,000 + 90,000 + 5,000 + 600 + 20 + 9 = 295,629 _____

    b. 900,000 + 50,000 + 2,000 + 3 = 950,203 _____

Roman Numerals

① Write each of the following in Roman numerals.

Symbol	Value
I	1
V	5
X	10
L	50
C	100
D	500
M	1,000

   a. 47 _____   **b.** 86 _____

   c. 99 _____   **d.** 368 _____

   e. 1,250 _____   **f.** 3,741 _____

② Write each of the following in digits.

   a. XXXIV _____   **b.** XLIII _____

   c. CCLX _____   **d.** MMC _____

   e. CDLXII _____   **f.** MCMX _____

③ Write the numbers in each of the following statements as Roman numerals.

   a. The clock's face only shows 3, 6, 9, and 12. _____

   b. We are 29 miles from Chicago. _____

   c. It is 78°F today. _____

   d. The movie was made in 2002. _____

   e. There are 14 pages in the newsletter. _____

   f. I was born in 1990. _____

④ Complete the patterns with Roman numerals.

   a. X, XX, XXX, _____, _____   **b.** L, LV, LX, _____, _____

   c. C, CC, CCC, _____, _____   **d.** M, MD, MM, _____, _____

⑤ Write the month, day, and year you were born in Roman numerals.

_____

⑥ Draw a clock face using Roman numerals and show the current time.

Addition Review

1 Add the following.

    a. 50 + 60 = _____   **b.** 90 + 30 = _____

    c. 40 + 80 = _____   **d.** 700 + 300 = _____

    e. 400 + 500 = _____   **f.** 700 + 800 = _____

2 Add the following.

    a. 129 + 66 = _____   **b.** 347 + 47 = _____

    c. 876 + 37 = _____   **d.** 247 + 38 = _____

    e. 164 + 29 = _____   **f.** 293 + 58 = _____

3 Give an estimate for each of the following by first rounding each number to the nearest hundred.

    a. 425 + 369 _____   **b.** 497 + 268 _____

    c. 876 + 281 _____   **d.** 979 + 319 _____

    e. 1,379 + 486 _____   **f.** 2,365 + 898 _____

4 Add the following.

    a.   487   **b.**   1,176   **c.**   4,158
         + 925   +   247   +4,925

    d.   8,436   **e.**   4,268   **f.**   5,281
      +5,219   +3,496   +2,986

5 Two country towns were merged together to form one town. If the two towns had populations of 27,846 and 39,468, what was the total population of the new town? _____

6 Write an addition word problem using the numbers 2,147 and 8,736 and then solve it.

_____

_____

❶ Add the following.

a.	4 6 0	b.	1 4 7	c.	9 7 6
	3 2 0		8 2 0		3 4 2
	+ 9 8 0		+ 4 7 6		+ 8 9 7

d.	1,2 4 8	e.	4,9 7 8	f.	7,8 5 6
	+ 3,6 8 7		+ 8,5 6 0		+ 9,2 7 8

❷ Add the following amounts.

a.	$ 4 6,2 7 5	b.	$ 4 9,3 2 5	c.	$ 5 6 1,1 0 1
	+ $ 1 2,3 8 6		+ $ 8 0,6 5 2		+ $ 2 9 9,9 8 0

d.	$ 9 2,1 4 6	e.	$ 7 5 9,7 0 4	f.	$ 1 2 4,9 8 0
	+ $ 8 6,4 5 6		+ $ 2 5,6 2 9		+ $ 8 9 3,2 7 6

❸ Give the missing numbers to complete the addition problems.

a.	3 5,_ 6 4	b.	6 3 2,_ _ _	c.	1 0 7,_ 3 _
	+ 4,8 _ 5		+ 2 0 1,2 6 4		+ _ 6 _,1 _ 7
	_ _,4 0 _		8 _ _,2 5 0		5 _ 3,1 1 9

d.	4 6 _,3 2 _	e.	3 2 _,1 8 _	f.	_ 2 _,8 _ 4
	+ 4 _ 2,_ _ 6		+ _ 6 2,_ 7 3		+ 2 _ 6,4 3 _
	_ 9 0,0 6 2		7 _ 1,9 _ 7		8 8 4,_ 9 1

❹ Solve the following.

a. Over 3 years, Albert saved $4,621, $3,283, and $2,146.
How much did Albert save altogether? _____

b. In a warehouse, one side had 46,291 boxes and the other
side had 39,472. How many boxes were there altogether? _____

c. There were 476 sheets of paper in one pile, 521 in a second, and
479 in a third. What was the total number of sheets of paper? _____

❺ Add: 942,100 + 38,617 + 12,496 + 10,748 _____

❻ Last year, Mr. Frank earned $57,975 at his job. This year,
Mr. Frank earned $60,545. How much has Mr. Frank
earned over the last two years? _____

Adding Large Numbers

1 Add the following.

a.	462,381	b.	849,106	c.	249,861
	942,117		283,427		248,105
	+107,437		+346,110		+624,177

d.	432,105	e.	406,109	f.	805,216
	869,117		841,086		34,975
	+348,052		+ 92,471		+ 98,647

2 Add the following.

a.	4,281,021	b.	486,325	c.	3,846,000	d.	840,000
	468,391		361,185		4,281,000		4,217,000
	+1,486,342		+1,428,593		+3,401,000		+8,673,000

3 Find the total of:

a. $426,831.50 and $217,856.93 _____

b. $1,024,309.25 and $4,629,326.54 _____

c. $5,029,859.98 and $6,254,321.40 _____

d. $1,500,450.10 and $900,428.50 _____

4 Find the total measurements. Include the units in your answer.

a. inches	4,980	b. pounds	46,832	c. feet	461,079
	6,243		10,976		213,461
	+10,479		+27,486		+874,982

5 Jorge bought a new car for $29,990 but added the navigation package for $1,755, better tires for $875, and a warranty for $2,465. What was the total cost of the car? _____

6 Add the following. Then rewrite your answer in words.

925,486.4
+106,432.7

_____

_____

Subtraction Review

❶ Subtract the following.

   a.   465
     − 38

   b.   890
     − 56

   c.   462
     − 88

   d.   436
     −175

   e.   248
     −109

   f.   756
     −237

❷ Subtract the following.

   a.   6,109
     −1,487

   b.   3,501
     −2,617

   c.   4,096
     −3,825

   d.   4,862
     −1,975

   e.   5,497
     −3,859

   f.   2,471
     −1,865

❸ Fill in the missing numbers.

   a.   5,617
     −4,_1_
     1,3_4

   b.   5,1_4
     −3,_27
     _,03_

   c.   9,5_1
     −_,_72
     6,86_

   d.   8,7_3
     −_,40_
     6,_55

   e.   8,_70
     − 7_3
     _,84_

   f.   8,_0_
     −_,0_4
     1,196

❹ Find the difference between the following numbers.

   a. 4,706 and 2,305 _____

   b. 8,975 and 1,723 _____

   c. 7,506 and 1,986 _____

   d. 5,630 and 146 _____

   e. 7,400 and 6,558 _____

   f. 3,248 and 967 _____

❺ If an item was bought for $2,385 and sold for $3,192, what was the profit made on the item? _____

❻ Nancy collects postage stamps. She has 246 stamps in her collection. If her book fits 793 stamps, how many more stamps can Nancy add to her stamp collection book? _____

Rounding Numbers

❶ Round each of the following to the nearest ten.

a. 47 _____

b. 63 _____

c. 98 _____

d. 114 _____

e. 256 _____

f. 486 _____

❷ Round each of the following to the nearest hundred.

a. 106 _____

b. 398 _____

c. 860 _____

d. 1,268 _____

e. 4,986 _____

f. 4,507 _____

❸ Round each of the following to the nearest thousand.

a. 986 _____

b. 1,046 _____

c. 2,793 _____

d. 17,600 _____

e. 29,826 _____

f. 126,108 _____

❹ Estimate an answer for each of the following by first rounding each number to the nearest thousand.

	Question	Rounded	Estimate
a.	5,778 + 3,697		
b.	2,866 + 3,105		
c.	1,249 + 2,958		
d.	35,977 + 6,104		
e.	55,394 + 5,106		
f.	9,999 + 27,108		

❺ *K* is used to represent 1,000 in large numbers. For example, 7,000 = 7K. Write each of the following using *K* as an abbreviation.

a. 9,000 _____

b. 14,000 _____

c. 21,000 _____

d. 51,000 _____

e. 37,000 _____

f. 85,000 _____

❻ True or false? To the nearest ten,:

a. 733 rounds to 730. _____

b. 964 rounds to 970. _____

c. 955 rounds to 950. _____

d. 827 rounds to 830. _____

1 Subtract the following.

a.	4 6 , 3 2 1	b.	5 2 , 1 8 7	c.	4 6 , 3 7 9
	− 9 , 8 6 0		− 7 , 9 5 0		− 8 , 6 6 0

d.	8 6 , 0 0 0	e.	3 9 , 8 7 0	f.	2 2 , 1 0 0
	− 5 1 , 3 6 0		− 1 4 , 6 0 0		− 1 7 , 8 5 0

2 Estimate the answer to each problem by first rounding each number to the nearest thousand in the space beside each one.

a.	4 6 , 7 8 5	b.	8 3 , 4 7 2
	− 2 1 , 3 9 1		− 6 7 , 9 5 7

c.	9 2 , 1 1 0	d.	6 6 , 8 5 2
	− 4 2 , 6 8 9		− 4 1 , 4 6 1

e.	5 9 , 8 5 0	f.	4 3 , 2 8 1
	− 1 7 , 0 8 2		− 1 0 , 9 2 5

3 Subtract the following measurements. Include the units in your answer.

a. inches	8 7 5 , 9 2 6	b. feet	4 9 1 , 2 5 3	c. miles	5 5 5 , 9 9 8
	− 3 2 1 , 5 2 0		− 1 2 4 , 6 8 5		− 4 3 2 , 5 6 5

4 Find the difference between the following numbers.

a. 924,685 and 143,847 _____   b. 462,398 and 120,801 _____

c. 502,196 and 475,230 _____   d. 673,895 and 421,114 _____

e. 794,503 and 306,040 _____   f. 526,807 and 304,752 _____

5 The profit from Saturday's rock concert was $846,217.
The profit from Sunday's rock concert was $783,504.
How much more profit did Saturday's rock concert earn? _____

6 Write a subtraction word problem that would result in an answer of 221,635.

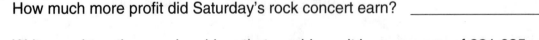

_____

_____

1 Subtract the following.

a.	1,683,000 − 429,000	b.	7,624,000 − 938,000	c.	5,280,000 −1,752,000

d.	4,630,000 −2,741,000	e.	8,049,000 −3,520,000	f.	1,946,000 − 897,000

2 Subtract the following amounts.

a.	$4,527,930 −$ 604,705	b.	$3,684,900 −$ 758,610	c.	$1,104,365 −$ 587,112

d.	$6,894,170 −$2,431,856	e.	$4,387,105 −$2,416,801	f.	$11,059,528 −$ 9,237,000

3 The area of eight states (including water) is given below in square miles.

Florida (FL) 65,755 mi.²	California (CA) 163,695 mi.²	Delaware (DE) 2,489 mi.²	Nevada (NV) 110,560 mi.²
Alaska (AK) 663,267 mi.²	**Hawaii (HI)** 10,931 mi.²	**Texas (TX)** 268,580 mi.²	**Oregon (OR)** 98,380 mi.²

Find the difference in area between:

a. FL and CA. _____   **b.** NV and HI. _____   **c.** TX and HI. _____

d. OR and DE. _____   **e.** AK and TX. _____   **f.** NV and OR. _____

4 Find:

a. 672,589 feet minus 361,876 feet. _____

b. the difference between $879,352 and $1,462,108. _____

c. 1,426,398 pounds take away 721,085 pounds. _____

5 What is the greatest difference in area between two states from question 3?

_____

6 In the box to the right, use all the digits from 1 through 7 to create two different 7-digit numbers. Then find the difference between the two.

Estimation

1 Estimate each sum by first rounding each number to the nearest hundred in the space beside each one.

a. 46,215
  +37,986

b. 17,580
  +19,271

c. 24,831
  +46,028

d. 142,853
  +173,127

e. 429,050
  +140,271

f. 873,056
  +117,820

2 Estimate each difference by first rounding each number to the nearest thousand in the space beside each one.

a. 42,107
  −19,658

b. 25,963
  − 7,631

c. 47,285
  −33,863

d. 129,427
  −114,306

e. 168,301
  −123,497

f. 850,176
  −327,871

3 Estimate each answer by first rounding each amount to the nearest dollar.

a. $421.95 + $62.35 _____

b. $121.75 + $156.85 _____

c. $643.06 + $249.16 _____

d. $479.15 − $135.66 _____

e. $846.27 − $137.98 _____

f. $649.29 − $377.88 _____

4 Estimate each sum by first rounding each number to the nearest hundred.

a. 4,267
  +1,958

b. 7,356
  +1,279

c. 8,791
  +4,076

d. 4,880
  +3,965

e. 6,217
  +7,463

f. 9,587
  + 998

5 Estimate the difference by first rounding each number to the nearest thousand.

  2,143,856
−1,794,301

6 Estimate the sum by first rounding each number to the nearest thousand.

  721,098
+385,175

Basic Multiplication

1 Multiply the following.

   a.   6   **b.**   1 0   **c.**   8
       × 4   × 6   × 9

   d.   3   **e.**   1 2   **f.**   0
       × 7   × 5   × 4

2 Find:

   a. 7 groups of 4. _____   **b.** 12 groups of 10. _____

   c. 8 groups of 5. _____   **d.** the product of 10 and 10. _____

   e. the product of 7 and 6. _____   **f.** the product of 9 and 4. _____

3 Find the missing numbers.

   a. $7 \times \boxed{} = 21$ **b.** $\boxed{} \times 10 = 90$ **c.** $8 \times \boxed{} = 64$

   d. $2 \times \boxed{} = 14$ **e.** $\boxed{} \times 5 = 20$ **f.** $\boxed{} \times 4 = 48$

4 Find the total cost of the following.

   a. 10 hats at \$9 each _____   **b.** 4 drinks at \$3 each _____

   c. 7 magazines at \$12 each _____   **d.** 3 bags of potatoes at \$5 each _____

   e. 12 snacks at \$2 each _____   **f.** 4 movie tickets at \$8 each _____

5 True or false?

   a. $6 \times 3 = 2 \times 9$ _____   **b.** $5 \times 7 = 3 \times 10$ _____

   c. $7 \times 7 = 5 \times 10$ _____   **d.** $12 \times 3 = 6 \times 6$ _____

   e. $10 \times 11 = 12 \times 10$ _____   **f.** $5 \times 8 = 4 \times 10$ _____

6 Complete the multiplication circle.

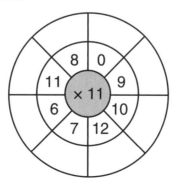

Multiplication Review

❶ Find:

    a. the product of 9 and 7. _____
    b. 8 groups of 2. _____

    c. 11 times 5. _____
    d. 12 multiplied by 12. _____

❷ Multiply the following.

    a.   1 2
         ×   8

    b.   6
        ×   0

    c.   4
        ×   7

    d.   5
        ×   9

    e.   7
        ×   5

    f.   3
        ×   2

❸ Find the missing numbers.

    a. $6 \times \boxed{} = \boxed{} = 12 \times 1$
  b. $9 \times \boxed{} = 72 = 6 \times \boxed{}$
  c. $\boxed{} \times 3 = \boxed{} = 6 \times 4$

    d. $6 \times 5 = \boxed{} = 3 \times \boxed{}$
  e. $2 \times 9 = \boxed{} = 6 \times \boxed{}$
  f. $5 \times \boxed{} = \boxed{} = 10 \times 2$

❹ Find the product. Write the answer in words.

    a. nine and three _____
    b. eight and six _____

    c. one and seven _____
    d. twelve and eleven _____

    e. twelve and nine _____
    f. zero and seven _____

❺ Find the total number of days in:

    a. 6 weeks. _____
    b. 2 weeks. _____

    c. 10 weeks. _____
    d. 3 weeks. _____

    e. 8 weeks. _____
    f. 7 weeks. _____

❻ Find the total number of animals if there were:

    • 5 fields with 12 cows in each

    • 2 fields with 3 horses in each

    • 2 pens with 2 pigs in each

    • 5 coops with 10 chickens in each   Total = _____

Multiplication of Tens, Hundreds, and Thousands

1 Find the following.

    a. 4 x 2 tens = _____ tens   **b.** 9 x 3 tens = _____ tens

    c. 6 x 7 hundreds = _____ hundreds   **d.** 5 x 5 hundreds = _____ hundreds

    e. 8 x 4 thousands = _____ thousands   **f.** 7 x 8 thousands = _____ thousands

2 Multiply the following.

    a.   40   **b.**   80   **c.**   600
         × 7   × 6   ×   9

    d.   500   **e.** 8,000   **f.** 6,000
        × 7   ×   4   ×   5

3 Multiply the following.

    a. 10 × 23 = _____   **b.** 10 × 14 = _____   **c.** 10 × 76 = _____

        20 × 23 = _____   20 × 14 = _____   20 × 76 = _____

        30 × 23 = _____   30 × 14 = _____   30 × 76 = _____

    d. 10 × 70 = _____   **e.** 10 × 40 = _____   **f.** 10 × 80 = _____

        20 × 70 = _____   20 × 40 = _____   20 × 80 = _____

        30 × 70 = _____   30 × 40 = _____   30 × 80 = _____

4 Complete the chart.

	x	10	100	1,000
a.	40			
b.	70			
c.	83			
d.	29			
e.	200			
f.	167			

5 Find the total number of the following.

    a. 4 boxes of 300 books each _____   **b.** 30 groups of 20 students each _____

    c. 40 stories of 90 words each _____   **d.** 423 bags of 100 pencils each _____

    e. 126 pages of 1,000 stars each _____   **f.** 47 bins of 1,000 balls each _____

6 The school shop ordered 20 boxes of snacks and
there were 89 snacks in each box. If 15 snacks
were sold from each box, how many were left in total? _____

Multiplication

1 Multiply the following.

a. 14
× 6

b. 19
× 3

c. 42
× 9

d. 37
× 5

e. 63
× 7

f. 81
× 4

2 Multiply the following.

a. 149
× 3

b. 258
× 4

c. 301
× 5

d. 825
× 6

e. 714
× 7

f. 552
× 8

3 Find the product of:

a. 4,311 and 2. _____

b. 2,481 and 3. _____

c. 8,051 and 4. _____

d. 1,192 and 5. _____

e. 5,352 and 6. _____

f. 1,052 and 7. _____

4 Multiply the following.

a. 4,860
× 3

b. 9,240
× 4

c. 1,070
× 5

d. 20,300
× 6

e. 43,000
× 9

f. 18,000
× 2

5 **a.** Find how many seconds in 1 hour. _____

b. How many seconds in 6 hours? _____

c. How many seconds in 10 hours? _____

6 Each night for one whole week, Jenny used 98 stickers while making a big art project. How many stickers did Jenny use for the art project by the end of the week? _____

Multiplication by 2-Digit Numbers

❶ Estimate the products of each of the following by first rounding the larger number to the nearest ten.

a.	258	b.	825	c.	714	d.	552
	× 4		× 6		× 7		× 8

❷ Find the following.

a. $13 \times 61 = (10 \times 61) + (3 \times 61) =$ _____

b. $23 \times 47 = (20 \times 47) + (3 \times 47) =$ _____

c. $29 \times 58 = (20 \times 58) + (9 \times 58) =$ _____

d. $32 \times 76 = (\_\times 76) + (\_\times 76) =$ _____

e. $17 \times 63 = (\_\times 63) + (\_\times 63) =$ _____

f. $43 \times 85 = (\_\times 85) + (\_\times 85) =$ _____

❸ Complete the following.

a. $27 \times 63 =$

63	63
×20	× 7

[ ] + [ ] = [ ]

b. $53 \times 87 =$

87	87
×50	× 3

[ ] + [ ] = [ ]

c. $37 \times 96 =$

96	96
×30	× 7

[ ] + [ ] = [ ]

d. $47 \times 26 =$

26	26
×40	× 7

[ ] + [ ] = [ ]

e. $22 \times 78 =$

78	78
×20	× 2

[ ] + [ ] = [ ]

f. $45 \times 53 =$

53	53
×40	× 5

[ ] + [ ] = [ ]

❹ Multiply the following.

a.	425	b.	572	c.	835
	× 30		× 60		× 50

d.	701	e.	259	f.	107
	× 33		× 26		× 47

❺ At Dream Denim clothing store, there were 231 pairs of jeans for sale at $35 each. If someone bought all these jeans, how much would it cost (before tax)? _____

❻ Find the answer to one thousand, one hundred twenty-six multiplied by thirty-seven. Write your answer in digits. _____

Extended Multiplication

1 Complete the following.

a. 4 × 30 = _____

40 × 30 = _____

400 × 30 = _____

b. 9 × 70 = _____

90 × 70 = _____

900 × 70 = _____

c. 60 × 20 = _____

600 × 20 = _____

6,000 × 20 = _____

2 Complete the following.

a.
```
      4 3
    × 2 5
```
_____ (5 × 4 3)

+ _____ (2 0 × 4 3)

b.
```
      7 3
    × 4 8
```
_____ (8 × 7 3)

+ _____ (4 0 × 7 3)

c.
```
      2 8
    × 7 5
```
_____ (___ × ___)

+ _____ (___ × ___)

d.
```
      3 7
    × 5 3
```
_____ (___ × ___)

+ _____ (___ × ___)

3 Multiply the following.

a.
```
   4,1 2 6
 ×       7
```

b.
```
   8,3 5 9
 ×       8
```

c.
```
     1 4 8
 ×     5 2
```

d.
```
     6 7 8
 ×     6 9
```

4 Complete the inventory table for the department store.

	Item	No. of Items	Cost of Each Item	Total Cost
a.	hats	98	$17	
b.	sunglasses	56	$89	
c.	pants	110	$48	
d.	T-shirts	126	$26	
e.	sandals	85	$32	
f.	shorts	92	$35	

5 Insert the missing numbers from the box into the correct calculations below.

27	32	65	26

a.
```
        9 2
    × [    ]
      1 8 4
  + 2,7 6 0
    2,9 4 4
```

b.
```
        4 7
    × [    ]
      2 3 5
  + 2,8 2 0
    3,0 5 5
```

c.
```
        7 2
    × [    ]
      4 3 2
  + 1,4 4 0
    1,8 7 2
```

d.
```
        6 9
    × [    ]
      4 8 3
  + 1,3 8 0
    1,8 6 3
```

6 Each month, Josh spends $32 for satellite TV service and $5 for a DVR. How much does he spend on TV services each year?

_____

Multiples, Factors, and Divisibility

1 Circle the numbers in each row that are evenly:

a.	divisible by 2.	302	491	682	1,105	6,234	8,255	95,253
b.	divisible by 3.	173	735	828	1,143	1,276	7,827	23,412
c.	divisible by 4.	423	536	984	1,364	1,649	6,385	26,424
d.	divisible by 5.	105	621	898	1,462	1,700	9,515	83,966
e.	divisible by 8.	256	452	984	1,076	1,935	6,456	73,265
f.	divisible by 9.	198	356	899	1,368	8,753	9,981	12,420

2 True or false?

a. 9 is a factor of 90 _____

b. 7 is a factor of 26 _____

c. 8 is a factor of 70 _____

d. 11 is a factor of 132 _____

e. 6 is a factor of 32 _____

f. 4 is a factor of 28 _____

3 List all the factors of:

a. 12: _____

b. 18: _____

c. 24: _____

d. 30: _____

e. 48: _____

f. 60: _____

4 Write down the first 8 multiples of:

a. 7: _____, _____, _____, _____, _____, _____, _____, _____

b. 6: _____, _____, _____, _____, _____, _____, _____, _____

c. 11: _____, _____, _____, _____, _____, _____, _____, _____

d. 12: _____, _____, _____, _____, _____, _____, _____, _____

e. 10: _____, _____, _____, _____, _____, _____, _____, _____

f. 8: _____, _____, _____, _____, _____, _____, _____, _____

5 Write the divisibility rule for 10. _____

6 List all the factors of 1,000. _____

_____

Estimating Products

❶ Round each first number to the nearest ten to make an estimate.

a. 31 × 6 _____   **b.** 49 × 7 _____

c. 53 × 5 _____   **d.** 103 × 9 _____

e. 204 × 8 _____   **f.** 298 × 4 _____

❷ Estimate the products by rounding each number to the nearest ten.

a. 82 × 21 _____   **b.** 47 × 29 _____

c. 43 × 63 _____   **d.** 38 × 19 _____

e. 54 × 67 _____   **f.** 31 × 72 _____

❸ Round each first number to the nearest ten and each second number to the nearest hundred to find an estimate.

a. 76 × 436 _____   **b.** 81 × 667 _____

c. 24 × 549 _____   **d.** 11 × 589 _____

e. 43 × 621 _____   **f.** 58 × 869 _____

❹ Estimate (E) the answer and then check with a calculator to find the actual (A) answer.

a. 623 × 47   E = _____   A = _____

b. 408 × 36   E = _____   A = _____

c. 89 × 127   E = _____   A = _____

d. 204 × 69   E = _____   A = _____

e. 579 × 23   E = _____   A = _____

f. 255 × 45   E = _____   A = _____

❺ Each week for 23 weeks, Sally delivered 379 newspapers. Estimate the total number of newspapers Sally delivered.

_____

❻ Brandon read 17 pages in his book every night for two weeks straight. Estimate the total number of pages Brandon read after two weeks.

_____

Division Practice

1 Complete the division equations using the multiplication equations.

a. $9 \times 8 = 72$

$72 \div 8 =$ _____

$72 \div 9 =$ _____

b. $6 \times 5 = 30$

$30 \div 5 =$ _____

$30 \div 6 =$ _____

c. $7 \times 4 = 28$

$28 \div 4 =$ _____

$28 \div 7 =$ _____

d. $12 \times 8 = 96$

$96 \div 8 =$ _____

$96 \div 12 =$ _____

e. $8 \times 6 = 48$

$48 \div 6 =$ _____

$48 \div 8 =$ _____

f. $3 \times 12 = 36$

$36 \div 3 =$ _____

$36 \div 12 =$ _____

2 Divide the following.

a. $81 \div 9 =$ _____

b. $24 \div 3 =$ _____

c. $10 \div 10 =$ _____

d. $40 \div 5 =$ _____

e. $49 \div 7 =$ _____

f. $90 \div 9 =$ _____

3 Use division to find the missing numbers.

a. $8 \times \boxed{} = 16$

b. $3 \times \boxed{} = 27$

c. $11 \times \boxed{} = 110$

d. $12 \times \boxed{} = 144$

e. $7 \times \boxed{} = 56$

f. $6 \times \boxed{} = 54$

4 Divide the following.

a. $2\overline{)64}$

b. $6\overline{)54}$

c. $8\overline{)96}$

d. $3\overline{)69}$

e. $4\overline{)88}$

f. $9\overline{)108}$

5 Josie has 164 pencils to put in 4 boxes evenly. How many pencils should she put in each box? _____

6 A group of 9 girls equally shared 45 donut holes. How many donut holes did each girl eat? _____

Division Review

1 Find one person's fair share if these soccer balls were shared among:

a. 4 boys. _____

b. 6 girls. _____

c. 8 students. _____

d. 2 teachers. _____

e. 12 parents. _____

f. 3 grandparents. _____

2 Find one share and the remainder, if the soccer balls from question 1 were shared among:

a. 5 boys. _____

b. 7 girls. _____

c. 9 parents. _____

d. 10 schools. _____

e. 20 teams. _____

f. 11 dogs. _____

3 Divide the following.

a. $180 \div 3 =$ _____

b. $450 \div 5 =$ _____

c. $240 \div 6 =$ _____

d. $350 \div 7 =$ _____

e. $400 \div 8 =$ _____

f. $360 \div 9 =$ _____

4 Complete the division table. An example has been done for you.

	Question	Quotient	Remainder
	$20 \div 3$	6	2
a.	$30 \div 4$		
b.	$51 \div 7$		
c.	$38 \div 4$		
d.	$40 \div 9$		
e.	$55 \div 10$		
f.	$63 \div 6$		

5 Complete the table by finding the missing number in each division question.

	Question	Quotient	Remainder
a.	___ $\div 6$	5	2
b.	___ $\div 8$	1	6
c.	___ $\div 3$	9	1
d.	___ $\div 7$	8	4

6 Write a division word problem that has a quotient of 7.

_____

_____

Division with Remainders

1 Divide the following.

    a. $52 \div 6 =$ _____

    b. $40 \div 3 =$ _____

    c. $70 \div 9 =$ _____

    d. $50 \div 11 =$ _____

    e. $80 \div 12 =$ _____

    f. $34 \div 4 =$ _____

2 Divide the following. These problems do not have remainders.

    a. $2\overline{)648}$

    b. $3\overline{)369}$

    c. $5\overline{)560}$

    d. $8\overline{)976}$

    e. $7\overline{)924}$

    f. $4\overline{)504}$

3 Divide the following.

    a. $10\overline{)722}$

    b. $10\overline{)655}$

    c. $5\overline{)547}$

    d. $8\overline{)2,644}$

    e. $3\overline{)9,026}$

    f. $9\overline{)2,735}$

4   **a.** Isabel has $465, which is 10 times as much as Katie has. How much does Katie have? _____

    b. 497 eggs have to be placed into cartons of 6. How many cartons will be completely filled? _____

    c. Each car needs 4 tires. If there is a pile of 639 tires, how many cars can be completed? _____

    d. 4,027 thumbtacks had to be put into 3 boxes equally. How many thumbtacks were there in each box? _____

5 Sara had 4 pieces of ribbon, each of different lengths: 48 cm, 38 cm, 52 cm, and 64 cm. What was the average length of the ribbon? _____

6 There were 5 dozen cupcakes at the bake sale. Seven customers bought cupcakes that day. At the end of the bake sale, there were 4 cupcakes left. If each customer bought the same number of cupcakes, how many did each one buy? _____

Division with Remainders — Fractions

1 How many whole pieces would each child receive if 5 children shared:

a. 5 pieces of fruit? _____   **b.** 6 pieces of fruit? _____   **c.** 10 pieces of fruit? _____

d. 7 pieces of fruit? _____   **e.** 12 pieces of fruit? _____   **f.** 23 pieces of fruit? _____

2 Divide the following and write each answer as a mixed number.

a. $2\overline{)43}$ **b.** $3\overline{)31}$ **c.** $4\overline{)29}$

d. $6\overline{)80}$ **e.** $5\overline{)94}$ **f.** $7\overline{)50}$

3 Divide the following and write each answer as a mixed number.

a. $6\overline{)902}$ **b.** $4\overline{)503}$ **c.** $7\overline{)629}$

d. $8\overline{)594}$ **e.** $9\overline{)256}$ **f.** $5\overline{)433}$

4 Divide the following and write each answer as a mixed number.

a. $6\overline{)7,265}$ **b.** $8\overline{)9,650}$ **c.** $3\overline{)5,471}$

d. $7\overline{)9,350}$ **e.** $9\overline{)2,468}$ **f.** $4\overline{)5,363}$

5 Divide the following and write each answer as a fraction.

a. $10\overline{)7}$ **b.** $4\overline{)1}$ **c.** $7\overline{)5}$

6 Divide two hundred forty-seven by three.
Write the answer as a mixed number. _____

❶ Divide the following.

a. $10\overline{)390}$ **b.** $10\overline{)850}$ **c.** $10\overline{)400}$

d. $10\overline{)671}$ **e.** $10\overline{)349}$ **f.** $10\overline{)850}$

❷ Divide the following.

a. $3\overline{)3,135}$ **b.** $5\overline{)5,055}$ **c.** $6\overline{)5,472}$

d. $8\overline{)9,616}$ **e.** $7\overline{)4,921}$ **f.** $4\overline{)8,360}$

❸ Divide the following. Write any remainders as fractions.

a. $4\overline{)2,013}$ **b.** $5\overline{)7,019}$ **c.** $3\overline{)1,605}$

d. $9\overline{)91,803}$ **e.** $8\overline{)70,615}$ **f.** $6\overline{)36,102}$

❹ **a.** 4,963 plants were planted in 7 rows. How many plants were there in each row?

_____

b. A band with 5 players earned $975. How much did each player receive?

_____

c. The same number of newspapers was placed in 8 piles. How many newspapers were there in each pile, if there were 1,656 newspapers to begin with?

_____

d. There are 4,563 chocolates to place in box trays. How many box trays are needed if 9 chocolates fit in each tray?

_____

❺ Find the missing number inside the division symbol. $5\overline{)}$ $\quad\dfrac{10,304 \text{ r3}}{}$

❻ How many weeks are in 8,407 days? _____

1 Divide the following. Write answers with remainders in decimal form.

a. 10)4,301

b. 10)7,438

c. 10)5,060

d. 10)8,497

e. 10)6,635

f. 10)9,010

2 Write the number of tens in the following numbers.

a. 4,369 _____

b. 21,070 _____

c. 46,000 _____

d. 21,040 _____

e. 39,110 _____

f. 61,270 _____

3 Divide the following. Write answers with remainders in decimal form.

a. 10)24,680

b. 10)71,020

c. 10)87,630

d. 10)190,416

e. 10)487,951

f. 10)847,315

4 There are 10 millimeters (mm) in each centimeter (cm). Change each of the following lengths to centimeters.

a. 9,600 mm _____

b. 17,500 mm _____

c. 490 mm _____

d. 8,710 mm _____

e. 38,420 mm _____

f. 1,120 mm _____

5 How many thousands are in 471,500? _____

6 Ten plastic stars fit in one box. How many boxes are filled if there are a total of 350,000 plastic stars? _____

Division by Numbers with Zeros

1 Divide the following.

    a. $10\overline{)5{,}760}$ **b.** $10\overline{)2{,}490}$ **c.** $10\overline{)3{,}100}$

    d. $10\overline{)23{,}000}$ **e.** $10\overline{)46{,}900}$ **f.** $10\overline{)48{,}700}$

2 Divide the following.

    a. $100\overline{)2{,}100}$ **b.** $100\overline{)3{,}700}$ **c.** $100\overline{)2{,}900}$

    d. $100\overline{)48{,}000}$ **e.** $100\overline{)52{,}000}$ **f.** $100\overline{)39{,}000}$

3 Complete by first dividing both numbers by 10.

    a. $50\overline{)1{,}050}$ **b.** $30\overline{)3{,}600}$ **c.** $40\overline{)2{,}800}$

    d. $70\overline{)42{,}000}$ **e.** $90\overline{)10{,}710}$ **f.** $60\overline{)1{,}800}$

4 Divide the following. Write remainders as fractions in simplest form.

    a. $90\overline{)3{,}033}$ **b.** $70\overline{)2{,}485}$ **c.** $60\overline{)2{,}142}$

    d. $80\overline{)7{,}632}$ **e.** $50\overline{)4{,}635}$ **f.** $40\overline{)7{,}288}$

5 Divide the following. Then, round each answer to the nearest whole number.

    a. $40\overline{)6{,}175}$ **b.** $50\overline{)8{,}432}$

6 Ten thousand, seven hundred people were placed into groups of 100. How many people were in each group?

    _____

❶ Divide the following.

a. $6\overline{)8,628}$ 　　　　b. $3\overline{)1,554}$ 　　　　c. $5\overline{)7,215}$

d. $4\overline{)1,936}$ 　　　　e. $8\overline{)8,496}$ 　　　　f. $7\overline{)7,245}$

❷ Divide the following.

a. $7\overline{)63,159}$ 　　　　b. $4\overline{)12,648}$ 　　　　c. $6\overline{)35,691}$

d. $10\overline{)42,681}$ 　　　　e. $9\overline{)71,463}$ 　　　　f. $5\overline{)42,183}$

❸ Solve the following.

a. How many students were at camp, if $\frac{1}{4}$ of 2,000 students were there? _____

b. 5,648 gallons divided into 8 large aquariums. _____

c. 746,325 ft.^{2} of land divided into 5 equal fields. _____

❹ Find the missing numbers inside the division symbols.

a. $3\overline{)}^{\,1,234}$ 　　　　b. $6\overline{)}^{\,1,021}$ 　　　　c. $7\overline{)}^{\,631}$

d. $9\overline{)}^{\,802}$ 　　　　e. $4\overline{)}^{\,2,116}$ 　　　　f. $8\overline{)}^{\,739}$

❺ If 396 points were scored in 6 games, what was the average number of points per game? _____

❻ Find the missing number. Inside the division symbol. $7\overline{)}^{\,2,413\ r5}$

Extended Division

① Complete the following. An example has been done for you.

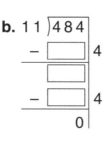

a. $12\overline{)288}$ = 24
- 24 | 2
- 48
- 48 | 4
- 0

b. $11\overline{)484}$
- ☐ | 4
- ☐
- ☐ | 4
- 0

c. $14\overline{)168}$
- ☐ | 1
- ☐
- ☐ | 2
- 0

d. $22\overline{)286}$
- ☐ | 1
- ☐
- ☐ | 3
- 0

② Use the above method to complete the following. Some include remainders.

a. $6\overline{)188}$ **b.** $13\overline{)496}$ **c.** $63\overline{)756}$ **d.** $27\overline{)290}$

③ Divide the following. Some include remainders

a. $299 \div 18 =$ _____   **b.** $600 \div 12 =$ _____

c. $496 \div 25 =$ _____   **d.** $147 \div 13 =$ _____

e. $735 \div 15 =$ _____   **f.** $78 \div 14 =$ _____

④ Find the missing numbers inside the division symbols.

a. $27\overline{)}$ 10 r 5

b. $14\overline{)}$ 46 r 2

c. $17\overline{)}$ 21 r 8

d. $57\overline{)}$ 24 r 1

⑤ How many cartons would 184 eggs fill if each carton holds one dozen eggs? How many eggs left over?   _____

⑥ If 416 blocks were equally sorted into 11 bins, how many blocks would be in each bin? How many blocks left over?   _____

Averages

1 Find the average of each group of numbers.

    a. 50 and 150 _____

    b. 125 and 200 _____

    c. 76, 14, 63, 22, 15 _____

    d. $10, $11.75, $12.15, $2.10 _____

    e. 5, 9, 13, 9, 17, 7 _____

    f. 7, 9, 13, 10, 9, 12, 10 _____

2 Below are the temperatures at 4:00 p.m. for one week. What is the average temperature at 4:00 p.m. for:

Day	Mon.	Tue.	Wed.	Thur.	Fri.	Sat.	Sun.
Temp °F	84	86	82	85	89	78	83

    a. Monday and Tuesday? _____

    b. Thursday and Friday? _____

    c. Tuesday, Wednesday, and Saturday? _____

    d. the weekend? _____

    e. Monday and Friday? _____

    f. the weekdays? _____

3 Find the average score for each of the hockey teams for the 6-game preseason.

	Team	Scores	Average
a.	Numbers	0, 3, 4, 2, 1, 2	
b.	Totals	6, 5, 2, 1, 3, 1	
c.	Dividers	0, 2, 1, 3, 0, 0	
d.	Multipliers	4, 6, 3, 7, 1, 3	
e.	Adders	5, 7, 3, 9, 1, 2	
f.	Subtracters	5, 6, 7, 8, 3, 4	

4 What is the average number of:

    a. marbles in jars of 112, 116, and 120? _____

    b. fruit in baskets of 7, 8, 19, 21, and 13? _____

    c. pencils in packets of 12, 10, 9, 10, 11, and 14? _____

    d. matches in boxes of 85, 72, 53, 107, and 92? _____

5 The average game score for eight games is 60. Find the missing score from game 3.

Game	1	2	3	4	5	6	7	8
Score	82	62		47	48	100	54	70

6 Find 3 numbers that give an average of 27. _____

Inverse Operations and Checking Answers

1 Use addition to check the subtraction equations. Mark an **X** in the box for those that are correct and write the correct answers for those that are incorrect.

a. $176 - 93 = 83$ ☐

b. $427 - 256 = 172$ ☐

c. $302 - 175 = 127$ ☐

d. $579 - 286 = 393$ ☐

e. $2,817 - 1,439 = 1,476$ ☐

f. $1,951 - 786 = 1,165$ ☐

2 Check the division equations. Mark an **X** in the box for those that are correct and write the correct answers for those that are incorrect.

a. $200 \div 10 = 2$ ☐

b. $420 \div 60 = 7$ ☐

c. $180 \div 60 = 90$ ☐

d. $100 \div 20 = 5$ ☐

e. $132 \div 11 = 12$ ☐

f. $840 \div 70 = 12$ ☐

3 Check the following statements. Answer *true* or *false*.

a. $126 + 235$ is less than 360 _____

b. 50×20 is greater than 900 _____

c. $800 \div 15$ is less than 50 _____

d. $1,246 - 728$ is more than 500 _____

e. 700×12 is less than 9,000 _____

f. $4,000 \div 20$ is greater than 250 _____

4 Match the inverse equations.

a. $6 \times ♥ = 150$

b. $40 \times ♥ = 120$

c. $♥ - 25 = 9$

d. $\frac{1}{2}$ of $♥ = 40$

e. $9 + ♥ = 25$

f. $6 + ♥ = 15$

A. $40 \times 2 = ♥$

B. $15 - 6 = ♥$

C. $♥ = 25 - 9$

D. $150 \div 6 = ♥$

E. $9 + 25 = ♥$

F. $120 \div 40 = ♥$

5 Jodie started with a number of pet birds; she sold 5 of them, bought 4 others, and then gave 3 away. She now has 12 birds. How many birds did Jodie have to start with? _____

6 Write an inverse equation to go with the below equation.

$12 = ▲ \div 8$ _____

Order of Operations

1 Solve the following. Complete the parentheses first, then multiplication and division, and finally addition and subtraction.

a. $(20 - 5) \times 10 =$ _____

b. $(7 + 5) \times 3 =$ _____

c. $6 \times (2 + 5) - 9 =$ _____

d. $(100 - 12 \times 3) \div 4 =$ _____

e. $(40 + 20) \div 5 + 15 =$ _____

f. $7 \times (5 + 6) =$ _____

2 Solve the following. Work left to right.

a. $9 \times 8 \div 2 =$ _____

b. $11 \times 6 \div 2 =$ _____

c. $60 \div 10 \times 3 =$ _____

d. $200 \div 4 \div 5 =$ _____

e. $4 \times 8 \times 2 \div 8 =$ _____

f. $12 \times 4 \div 6 =$ _____

3 Solve the following. Complete the multiplication and division first.

a. $20 + 3 \times 5 =$ _____

b. $30 - 12 \div 4 + 14 =$ _____

c. $200 - 12 \times 12 =$ _____

d. $26 + 5 \times 7 + 19 =$ _____

e. $36 + 84 \div 4 - 50 =$ _____

f. $46 - 66 \div 3 =$ _____

4 Solve the following. Complete the parentheses first, then multiplication and division, and finally addition and subtraction.

a. $(4 + 6) \times 9 - 38 =$ _____

b. $(10 - 7) \times 5 - 2 \times 6 =$ _____

c. $7 \times 4 + 50 \div 2 =$ _____

d. $47 + 10 \times (12 + 3) =$ _____

e. $(400 \div 10) \div (5 \times 4) =$ _____

f. $52 + (7 + 9) \div 4 =$ _____

5 Solve the following.

a. $36 \div 9 \times 4 + 6 =$ _____

b. $(36 \div 9) \times (4 + 6) =$ _____

c. $36 \div (9 \times 4) + 6 =$ _____

d. $(32 - 4) \times (5 \times 10) + 22 =$ _____

e. $(32 - 4) \times 5 \times (10 + 22) =$ _____

f. $320 - 4 \times 5 \times 10 + 22 =$ _____

6 Add two sets of parentheses to make the below equation true.

$$17 + 3 + 5 \times 4 = 16 - 7 + 8 \times 5$$

Order of Operations with Decimals and Fractions

❶ Solve the following. Complete the parentheses first. Write answers as decimals.

a. $(5 + 2) \times \frac{1}{2} =$ _____

b. $\frac{1}{4} \times (7 + 5) =$ _____

c. $2 \times 6 \div (12 - 2) =$ _____

d. $(4.3 + 2.7) \times 3 =$ _____

e. $(1.9 + 0.1) \div 2 =$ _____

f. $0.5 \times (6 + 12) - 3 =$ _____

❷ Solve the following. Work left to right.

a. $44 \times 2 \div 8 =$ _____

b. $2 \times x \times 4 \div 2 =$ _____

c. $2.8 \div 4 \times 2 =$ _____

d. $3.6 \div 6 \times 2 =$ _____

e. $4.2 \times 4 \div 2 =$ _____

f. $5.5 \times 7 \div 5 =$ _____

❸ Solve the following. Do multiplication and division before addition and subtraction.

a. $3.2 \times 5 + 6.1 \times 2 =$ _____

b. $60 + 9.3 \times 4 + 12.3 =$ _____

c. $14.4 \div 12 + 3.8 =$ _____

d. $20 - 8.1 \div 3 + 4.6 =$ _____

e. $2 \times 6.2 + 5.5 \div 5 =$ _____

f. $100 \div 0.5 - 50 \times 2.5 =$ _____

❹ Solve the following. Complete the parentheses first, then multiplication and division, and finally addition and subtraction.

a. $(\frac{3}{9} + \frac{2}{3}) \times 7 =$ _____

b. $(\frac{1}{2} \times 6) \div (\frac{1}{4} \times 20) =$ _____

c. $\frac{1}{8} \times (16 + 8) =$ _____

d. $4 - (\frac{2}{10} + \frac{3}{10}) + 1\frac{1}{2} =$ _____

e. $(8 + 3) \div 4 =$ _____

f. $(9\frac{3}{5} - \frac{3}{5}) \times 5 =$ _____

❺ Solve the following.

a. $(2 + 3) \times \frac{1}{5} =$ _____

b. $2 + (3 \times \frac{1}{5}) =$ _____

c. $7.5 \times 2 \div 3 =$ _____

d. $40 - 4 \times 9.3 + 7.3 =$ _____

❻ Add one set of parentheses to make the below equation true.

$$0.4 + 0.3 \times 12 - 0.2 - 1.0 = 7.2$$

Mixed Operations

1 Solve the following.

a. 725 − 346 + 107 = _____

b. $\frac{3}{4} + \frac{5}{4} - 2 =$ _____

c. 436 − 109 + 241 + 6 = _____

d. (405 + 107) − (99 + 32) = _____

e. 0.9 + 1.1 + 4.3 − 2.9 = _____

f. 8,246 + 1,097 − 5,559 = _____

2 Solve the following.

a. (9 × 2) ÷ 3 = _____

b. (100 ÷ 2) × 14 = _____

c. (10 × 10) ÷ (4 × 5) = _____

d. (50 ÷ 5) × (2 × 5) = _____

e. 4 × 6 × 7 × 0 = _____

f. 90 ÷ 9 × (7 × 8) = _____

3 Solve the following.

a. (4 x 4) ÷ (2 + 6) = _____

b. (107 − 98) ÷ 3 = _____

c. (102 + 47) − 100 ÷ 2 = _____

d. $\frac{1}{2}$ × 50 + 32 = _____

e. (4.2 x 3) + (4.8 ÷ 6) = _____

f. (146 + 23) ÷ 13 = _____

4 Write each of the following as an equation.

a. *M* is 10 more than the product of 7, 3, and 2. _____

b. *Z* is the sum of 16, 17 and 18, divided by 3. _____

c. If I add 11 and 9, divide by 4, and multiply by 7, my answer is *K*. _____

d. *H* is the answer to 11 multiplied by 12, divided by 2, then 4 added. _____

5 Solve the equations from question 4 to find the value of each letter.

a. M = _____

b. Z = _____

c. K = _____

d. H = _____

6 Solve for *N*.

9.8 divided by 2, 0.1 added, and the result divided by 8 gives *N*.

N = _____

Zero in Operations

① Solve the following.

   a. $4 \times 16 \times 3 \times 0 =$ _____

   b. $1{,}000 \times 7 \times 0 =$ _____

   c. $(4 + 9 + 7) \times 0 =$ _____

   d. $(46 - 9) \times 0 =$ _____

   e. $(42 \div 7) \times (5 - 5) =$ _____

   f. $(9 - 9) \times (100 \div 5) =$ _____

② Add or subtract the following.

a.	**b.**	**c.**
428,199	247,100	4,750,000
360,400	836,900	2,180,000
+901,000	+100,000	+4,603,000

d.	**e.**	**f.**
450,000	876,000	64,000,000
−263,000	− 98,500	− 2,750,000

③ Multiply or divide the following.

a.	**b.**	**c.**
410,270	694,200	8,391,000
× 3	× 7	× 8

   d. $4{\overline{\smash{)}107{,}400}}$
   e. $5{\overline{\smash{)}7{,}632{,}000}}$
   f. $10{\overline{\smash{)}3{,}623{,}000}}$

④ Complete the missing numbers in the blanks.

   a.   1 0 _ , 7 6 _
     + 3 2 8 , _ _ 7
     _ _ 0 , 0 9 7

   b.   4 , 7 1 _ , 9 _ 4
     − 1 , _ 6 4 , _ 8 _
     _ , 0 4 8 , 3 1 0

   c.   1 _ _ , _ 8 0
     $5{\overline{\smash{)}\,\_\,9\,3{,}4\,\_\,\_}}$

   d.   _ 0 7
     × 4 _
     2 , 1 4 9
     + 1 2 , _ _ _
     _ _ , _ _ _

⑤ A company makes 946,000 bags of potato chips every month. How many bags of potato chips are made in one year? _____

⑥ Steve, Larry, and Mike played in the Big Money Game Show. They each won a lot of money in the game. Steve won $416,700, Larry won $293,800, and Mike won $460,000. What is the difference between the greatest and the least winnings?

_____

Equations

1 Solve for each variable in the following equations.

    a. $M - 9 = 42$ _____

    b. $95 \div 5 = W$ _____

    c. $10 \times 10 = V^2$ _____

    d. $D - 3.2 = 6$ _____

    e. $50 + K = 76$ _____

    f. $9 \times A = 100 - 37$ _____

2 Solve each of the following equations.

    a. $\frac{1}{2} \times 40 + 1 = B$ _____

    b. $C = (5 \times 10) + (18 \div 3)$ _____

    c. $E = 36 \div (3 \times 2)$ _____

    d. $T = (49 \div 7) + 20$ _____

    e. $(3 \times 15) - (2 \times 5) = Z$ _____

    f. $(32 \times 9) \div (12 \times 12) = Y$ _____

3 Solve for each variable in the following equations.

    a. $81 \div N = 27$ _____

    b. $30 - 5 = 17 + H$ _____

    c. $8.5 + P = 10$ _____

    d. $\frac{1}{4} \times R = 40$ _____

    e. $20 - S = 16.3$ _____

    f. $\frac{1}{6} + F = \frac{1}{2}$ _____

4 Write an equation for each of the following. Use *G* for each unknown number.

    a. Five friends went to the movies. If the total cost of the tickets was $42.50, how much did each ticket cost? _____

    b. Arthur had some apples, 4 bananas, and 6 plums. If he had 13 pieces of fruit, how many apples did he have? _____

    c. The chocolates were divided into 4 rows of 3 for each tray. If there are 60 chocolates, how many trays are needed? _____

    d. In the garden, there are 5 rows of 7 tomato plants and 6 rows of lettuce plants. If there are 71 plants altogether, how many plants are in each row of lettuce? _____

5 Solve the equations from question 4 to find the value of each unknown.

    a. $G =$ _____

    b. $G =$ _____

    c. $G =$ _____

    d. $G =$ _____

6 I take a number, divide by the sum of seven and three, add fifty, and subtract seven. If I end up at the number that is equal to nine multiplied by five, what number did I begin with? _____

Operations with Money

❶ Round each of the following amounts to the nearest 5 cents.

    a. $4.73 _____   **b.** $2.99 _____   **c.** $81.67 _____

    d. $100.02 _____   **e.** $3.44 _____   **f.** $1,010.89 _____

❷ Add or subtract the following amounts.

    a. $ 9.6 5
          $ 2.3 5
      + $ 1.0 7

    b. $ 6.7 5
          $ 2.9 8
      + $ 4.5 5

    c. $ 8.5 5
          $ 6.3 2
      + $ 1.9 9

    d. $ 4.2 0
      − $ 3.9 8

    e. $ 85.9 1
      − $ 76.4 5

    f. $ 1 1 2.6 2
      − $ 9 8.8 5

❸ Multiply or divide the following.

    a. $ 6.4 0
      ×   5

    b. $ 9.2 9
      ×   7

    c. $ 4.3 5
      ×   9

    d. 3)$ 8.5 5

    e. 5)$ 1 2.7 5

    f. 4)$ 9.5 6

❹ Find the change from $14.50 if Jane spent:

    a. $9.85 _____   **b.** $3.95 _____   **c.** $4.20 _____

    d. $8.47 _____   **e.** $12.79 _____   **f.** $10.65 _____

❺ Find the total cost of 3 pounds of apples, 4 pounds of bananas, and 2 pounds of oranges according to the prices below.

Oranges	Bananas	Apples
$1.45/lb.	$0.99/lb.	$2.25/lb.

_____

❻ Travis bought 2 of the exact same shirts—one for himself and the other for his twin brother, Tom. The total for the shirts was $15.48. Tom did not like the shirt that Travis bought for him, so Travis returned one shirt to the store. How much money did Travis get back?

_____

❶ Find the value of each letter.

a. $d + d + d + d = 120$ _____

b. $Y + 6 = 20$ _____

c. $s \times s \times s = 27$ _____

d. $T + T = 50$ _____

e. $\frac{1}{4}$ of $W = 12$ _____

f. $m^2 = 81$ _____

❷ Write an equation for each of the following and solve.

a. multiply 5 by 100, and subtract six times seven _____

b. divide 49 by 7, and then add the product of eight and two _____

c. add 15 to nine, multiply by three, and then divide by eight _____

d. to 11.9, add 6 before subtracting 9.3 _____

e. square 5, and multiply by the product of 4 and 1 _____

f. divide 22 in half and multiply by 12, and then add eight _____

❸ Solve the following.

a. $(5 \times 3) + (7 \times 11) =$ _____

b. $(10 \times 6) \div (5 \div 1) =$ _____

c. $3 \times (1.5 + 2.6) =$ _____

d. $49 \times 10 - (8 \times 12) =$ _____

e. $15 \times 6 + 39 =$ _____

f. $(100 - 70) \times 4 =$ _____

❹ Complete the table.

▲	2.3	6	7.8	9.05
■	1.7	4.2	**d.**	6.11
▲ + ■	**a.**	**c.**	11.3	15.16
▲ − ■	**b.**	1.8	**e.**	**f.**

❺ Solve each equation, and then match the correct equation to the diagram.

a. $24 - 3 \times 4 =$ _____

b. $9 \times 2 - 7 =$ _____

c. $2.5 \times 4 =$ _____

d. $7.3 + 3.7 =$ _____

❻ The cost of the football was $25.50 plus sales tax. If the total cost was $27.25, how much was the tax? Write an equation and solve for the answer.

_____

Substituting Values

❶ Write *true* or *false* for each of the given answers.

a. $(8 \times \blacktriangle) + 4 = 20$
   $\blacktriangle = 2$ _____

b. $17 + (3 \times \blacktriangle) = 34$
   $\blacktriangle = 5$ _____

c. $(9 \div \blacktriangle) \times 3 = 27$
   $\blacktriangle = 1$ _____

d. $41 - (6 \times \blacktriangle) = 18$
   $\blacktriangle = 4$ _____

e. $(4 + \blacktriangle) \times 2 = 40$
   $\blacktriangle = 18$ _____

f. $41 - (6 \times \blacktriangle) = 18$
   $\blacktriangle = 5$ _____

❷ Find the missing number in each question.

a. $\boxed{} - 42 = 35$

b. $\boxed{} + 311 = 500$

c. $4 \times \boxed{} = 64$

d. $\boxed{} \div 3 = 60$

e. $(5 \times \boxed{}) + 29 = 59$

f. $(\boxed{} \div 5) + 10 = 20$

❸ Find the missing number in each of the following.

a.
```
    6 0 7
+ [      ]
  ─────────
  1 , 3 8 9
```

b.
```
  4 , 3 2 6
- [      ]
  ─────────
  3 , 5 3 7
```

c.
```
      4 6 1
×   [    ]
  ─────────
  3 , 2 2 7
```

d.
```
    1 , 5 6 2
2) [        ]
```

e.
```
      9 5 6
+ [      ]
  ─────────
  1 , 7 3 4
```

f.
```
  2 6 3 , 9 0 0
- [          ]
  ─────────────
  1 1 7 , 4 0 0
```

❹ Find the number (N) if I:

a. double it, then add 6. The answer is 50. _____

b. multiply by 7, then subtract 15. The answer is 62. _____

c. add 100, then divide by 5. The answer is 40. _____

d. subtract 13, then multiply by 3. The answer is 237. _____

e. divide it in half, then subtract 57. The answer is 50. _____

f. divide it by 3, add 47. The answer is 69. _____

❺ Find all the different pairs of whole numbers that will make the number sentence true.

$46 - 28 = \blacksquare \times \blacktriangle$ _____

❻ Colorful erasers were equally placed in 8 boxes. If there was a total of 9,872 erasers, how many were in each box? Write an equation and solve for the answer.

_____

Number Sentences

1 Write *true* or *false* for each of the following.

   a. $100 \div ♥ + 5 = 30$ $♥ = 4$ _____

   b. $20 - (5 \times ♥) = 5$ $♥ = 3$ _____

   c. $20 - ♥ = 18.2$ $♥ = 2.8$ _____

   d. $(90 + ♥) \times \frac{1}{2} = 20$ $♥ = 10$ _____

2 Find the value of each of the missing numbers.

   a. $9 \times \boxed{} = 60 + 3$ **b.** $24 \div 3 = 2 \times \boxed{}$ **c.** $49 - \boxed{} = 5 \times 6$

   d. $56 + 12 = 80 - \boxed{}$ **e.** $19 - \boxed{} = 18 \times 1$ **f.** $400 \div 20 = 7 + \boxed{}$

3 Check if each of the following is correct. Write *true* for those that are correct. Write *false* and then correct those that are wrong.

   a. James bought 15 bags of cement at $9 per bag.
   He spent $145 in total.   _____

   b. Andy divided 92 bottles into 4 crates. There were
   24 bottles in each crate.   _____

   c. 84 treats were shared among 6 dogs. Each dog
   received 14 treats.   _____

   d. There were 412 letters for delivery. By lunchtime,
   256 had been delivered. 146 letters still needed
   to be delivered.   _____

4 Construct a number sentence for each of the problems and solve for each, using *N* as the unknown number.

   a. the product of 8 and a number is 24 _____

   b. the quotient of a number and 4 is 12 _____

   c. a number is decreased by 17, resulting in 45 _____

   d. a number is squared, then 9 is added to get 90 _____

5 Find the value of # in each of the following.

   a. $\# \div 3 = 1.1$ _____   **b.** $\# - \frac{3}{4} = \frac{3}{4}$ _____   **c.** $14 + \# = 16.2$ _____

   d. $\# - 6 = \frac{3}{8}$ _____   **e.** $9 \times \# = 9.9$ _____   **f.** $6 + \# = 11.7$ _____

6 Create your own number sentences by placing a number in each box. Make sure each number sentence is true.

   a. $\boxed{} - \boxed{} = \boxed{} \times \boxed{}$ **b.** $\boxed{} + \boxed{} = \boxed{} - \boxed{} \div \boxed{}$

Square and Cube Numbers

❶ Complete the following.

a. $9 \times 9 =$ _____

b. $20 \times 20 =$ _____

c. $14 \times 14 =$ _____

d. $3 \times 3 \times 3 =$ _____

e. $10 \times 10 \times 10 =$ _____

f. $4 \times 4 \times 4 =$ _____

❷ Square or cube each number as marked.

a. $8^2 =$ _____

b. $6^3 =$ _____

c. $7^2 =$ _____

d. $5^3 =$ _____

e. $12^2 =$ _____

f. $20^3 =$ _____

❸ Complete the table by squaring and cubing each number.

	a.	**b.**	**c.**	**d.**	**e.**	**f.**
Number	1	2	3	4	5	6
Squared						
Cubed						

❹ Solve the following.

a. $4^2 + 3^2 =$ _____

b. $2^2 - 1^2 =$ _____

c. $9^2 - 5^2 =$ _____

d. $4^2 + 5^2 =$ _____

e. $12^2 - 8^2 =$ _____

f. $7^2 + 1^2 + 3^2 =$ _____

❺ Complete the following to discover the pattern. Write the pattern below.

a. $2^2 - 1^2 =$ _____

b. $3^2 - 2^2 =$ _____

c. $4^2 - 3^2 =$ _____

d. $5^2 - 4^2 =$ _____

e. $6^2 - 5^2 =$ _____

f. $7^2 - 6^2 =$ _____

Pattern: _____

❻ Bobby wrote his information in code below. Break the code and rewrite Bobby's information.

a. Address = 16^3 Emerald Street _____

b. Birthday = September 5^2, ($12^3 + 267$) _____

c. Phone Number = 27^2 18^3 _____

1 Use <, >, or = to make each number statement true.

   a. 12,000,100 ☐ 1,210,200   **b.** 20,000,000 ☐ 15,000,000

   c. 9,637,210 ☐ 9,367,219   **d.** 750,000 ☐ 75,000 × 100

   e. 10,000 × 100 ☐ 1,000,000   **f.** 23,000,461 ☐ 2,397,246

2 Write the whole number that is:

   a. immediately after 46,201,499. _____   **b.** 1,000 greater than 46,789,208. _____

   c. 5 more than 21,698._____   **d.** immediately before 400,000. _____

   e. 10,000 less than 245,306,200. _____   **f.** 1,000,000 more than 26,486,295. _____

3 A car's owner's manual says to change the oil every 5,000 miles. Record the odometer readings for when the next two oil changes will be required for each of the different cars below.

   a. Car 1: 11,428 miles,_____ miles, and_____ miles

   b. Car 2: 4,986 miles, _____ miles, and_____ miles

   c. Car 3: 46,725 miles, _____ miles, and_____ miles

   d. Car 4: 95,675 miles, _____ miles, and_____ miles

4 Complete the next line in the tree diagram for each of the following.

   a.   400   **b.**   1,000   **c.**   256

       2 0 × 2   250 × 4   8 × 3 2

     ☐ × ☐   ☐ × ☐ ☐ × ☐   ☐ × ☐ ☐ × ☐

   d.   96   **e.**   450   **f.**   1,400

       6 × 1 6   1 8 × 2 5   5 0 × 2 8

    ☐ × ☐ ☐ × ☐   ☐ × ☐ ☐ × ☐   ☐ × ☐ ☐ × ☐

5 In the number 4,683,251.07, which digit:

   a. has the greatest value? _____   **b.** means $\frac{7}{100}$? _____

   c. will change when 100,000 is added? _____

6 Complete a horizontal factor tree for the number 9,000.

   9,000 <

Negative Numbers

1 Place each set of numbers in ascending order.

   a. 3, -3, 1, -5, 0, -2, -1, 4, 6 _____

   b. -10, 1, -5, 0, 2, 5, -3, -1, 6 _____

   c. 2, 4, 0, -2, -4, -6, 6 _____

2 Place each set of numbers in descending order.

   a. -1, -3, 5, 0, 3, -5, 1, 7 _____

   b. -20, 10, 20, -30, -15, -10, 0, 5 _____

   c. 19, 18, 14, 13, 0, -10, 15, -15, -13, -6 _____

3 On June 30th, the temperature was 85°F. What would the temperature be on July 1st if it was:

   a. 4 degrees warmer? _____   **b.** 5 degrees cooler? _____

   c. 2 degrees colder? _____   **d.** 10 degrees hotter? _____

   e. 7 degrees colder? _____   **f.** 11 degrees colder? _____

4 Adam had $25 in his bank account. What would his bank balance be if he wrote a check for:

   a. $20? _____   **b.** $17? _____   **c.** $25? _____

   d. $30? _____   **e.** $49? _____   **f.** $82? _____

5 Display each "jump" in the following equations on the number lines to solve each one.

   a. $7 + 3 - 6 - 7 - 2 =$ _____

   b. $10 - 5 - 2 - 4 + 6 =$ _____

   c. $0 - 3 + 2 + 9 - 1 =$ _____

   d. $-4 + 2 - 6 + 7 - 1 =$ _____

6 Solve each equation.

   a. $-10 + 10 - 7 + 7 + 3 =$ _____   **b.** $0 - 2 + 5 + 6 =$ _____

   c. $-2 + 3 - 8 - 2 + 1 =$ _____   **d.** $5 - 2 - 6 + 4 + 1 =$ _____

Prime and Composite Numbers

1 Identify which of the following are prime (p) and which are composite (c) numbers.

a. 91 _____   b. 63 _____   c. 13 _____

d. 71 _____   e. 58 _____   f. 83 _____

2 Circle the numbers in the chart that are evenly divisible by the given divisor.

	Divisor	Possible Numbers					
a.	2	16	38	91	156	344	1,029
b.	3	21	54	80	122	225	1,471
c.	4	40	88	102	164	490	1,562
d.	5	60	76	95	120	581	1,247
e.	6	72	90	110	149	684	1,436
f.	7	77	105	149	196	485	1,260

3 Find two prime numbers that add up to the following sums.

a. 78 _____   b. 24 _____

c. 100 _____   d. 60 _____

e. 30 _____   f. 90 _____

4 Write three composite numbers between, but not including, the following numbers.

a. 5 and 15 _____   b. 17 and 24 _____

c. 50 and 60 _____   d. 80 and 100 _____

e. 115 and 125 _____   f. 150 and 160 _____

5 List all the prime numbers less than 50. _____

_____

6 In the space at the right, write a subtraction problem following the sample below and solve it.

    4-digit composite number
– 2-digit prime number
_____

Fractions

1 What part of each of the following shapes has been shaded?

a. 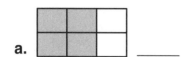 _____

b.  _____

c. 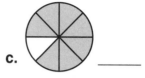 _____

d. 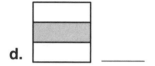 _____

e. _____

f. _____

2 What part of each shape in question 1 has **not** been shaded?

a. _____

b. _____

c. _____

d. _____

e. _____

f. _____

3 Shade each shape to show the given fraction.

a. $\frac{4}{8}$

b. $\frac{1}{4}$

c. $\frac{9}{10}$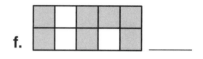

d. $\frac{2}{5}$

e. $\frac{1}{2}$

f. $\frac{5}{6}$

4 What part of each group has been shaded?

a.  ____

b.  ____

c.  ____

d.  ____

e. ____

f. ____

5 In the space below, draw groups of shapes and shade them to represent the following.

a. $\frac{2}{3}$ of the circles

b. $\frac{4}{7}$ of the squares

c. $\frac{2}{9}$ of the triangles

6 If $\frac{3}{4}$ of a set of pencils are broken, and there are

24 pencils in a set, how many pencils are **not** broken? _____

Fraction of a Group

1 Find the number of balls for each fraction.

   a. $\frac{1}{3}$ = ____

   b. $\frac{1}{4}$ = ____

   c. $\frac{1}{2}$ = ____

   d. $\frac{1}{6}$ = ____

   e. $\frac{3}{4}$ = ____

   f. $\frac{4}{6}$ = ____

2 Find and shade the fraction of each group.

   a. $\frac{1}{3}$ of 6 = ____

   b. $\frac{1}{4}$ of 16 = ____

   c. $\frac{1}{5}$ of 10 = ____

   d. $\frac{1}{2}$ of 8 = ____

   e. $\frac{1}{6}$ of 18 = ____

   f. $\frac{1}{4}$ of 20 = ____

3 Find the fraction of each group.

   a. $\frac{1}{4}$ of 48 = ____

   b. $\frac{1}{10}$ of 110 = ____

   c. $\frac{1}{3}$ of 60 = ____

   d. $\frac{3}{4}$ of 100 = ____

   e. $\frac{3}{8}$ of 32 = ____

   f. $\frac{3}{5}$ of 80 = ____

4   **a.** The used car lot had 120 cars. $\frac{1}{6}$ were sold. How many cars were sold? _____

   b. Ann had 50 fan letters and she replied to $\frac{4}{5}$ of them. How many did she still have to reply to? _____

   c. Rose had 130 emails. She had replied to $\frac{7}{10}$ of them. How many did she reply to? _____

   d. A concert special on TV went for $\frac{7}{12}$ of an hour. How many minutes did it go for? _____

5 In the space below, draw a small diagram for each of the following and solve.

   a. $\frac{3}{5}$ of 15 = ____

   b. $\frac{2}{3}$ of 18 = ____

6 On the test, Mark said $\frac{4}{5}$ of 90 is 74. Was he right? Explain. _____

Equivalent Fractions

❶ Complete to make each of the following equivalent fractions.

a. $\dfrac{5}{6} \dfrac{(\times 2)}{(\times 2)} = \dfrac{\square}{\square}$

b. $\dfrac{1}{10} \dfrac{(\times 5)}{(\times 5)} = \dfrac{\square}{\square}$

c. $\dfrac{2}{3} \dfrac{(\times 4)}{(\times 4)} = \dfrac{\square}{\square}$

d. $\dfrac{1}{6} \dfrac{(\times 10)}{(\times 10)} = \dfrac{\square}{\square}$

e. $\dfrac{3}{4} \dfrac{(\times 3)}{(\times 3)} = \dfrac{\square}{\square}$

f. $\dfrac{4}{5} \dfrac{(\times 6)}{(\times 6)} = \dfrac{\square}{\square}$

❷ Complete the equivalent fractions.

a. $\dfrac{2}{4} \dfrac{(\div 2)}{(\div 2)} = \dfrac{\square}{\square}$

b. $\dfrac{5}{10} \dfrac{(\div 5)}{(\div 5)} = \dfrac{\square}{\square}$

c. $\dfrac{6}{8} \dfrac{(\div 2)}{(\div 2)} = \dfrac{\square}{\square}$

d. $\dfrac{9}{15} \dfrac{(\div 3)}{(\div 3)} = \dfrac{\square}{\square}$

e. $\dfrac{10}{15} \dfrac{(\div 5)}{(\div 5)} = \dfrac{\square}{\square}$

f. $\dfrac{12}{24} \dfrac{(\div 6)}{(\div 6)} = \dfrac{\square}{\square}$

❸ What number has been used to multiply the numerator and the denominator in each of the following pairs of equivalent fractions?

a. $\dfrac{1}{6} = \dfrac{2}{12}$ _____

b. $\dfrac{1}{3} = \dfrac{4}{12}$ _____

c. $\dfrac{1}{5} = \dfrac{2}{10}$ _____

d. $\dfrac{3}{4} = \dfrac{6}{8}$ _____

e. $\dfrac{1}{4} = \dfrac{3}{12}$ _____

f. $\dfrac{2}{3} = \dfrac{4}{6}$ _____

❹ Find the missing number in each equivalent fraction.

a. $\dfrac{1}{2} = \dfrac{\square}{8}$

b. $\dfrac{2}{3} = \dfrac{\square}{6}$

c. $\dfrac{1}{3} = \dfrac{4}{\square}$

d. $\dfrac{2}{5} = \dfrac{10}{\square}$

e. $\dfrac{2}{3} = \dfrac{6}{\square}$

f. $\dfrac{3}{5} = \dfrac{9}{\square}$

❺ Write *true* or *false* for each of the following.

a. $\dfrac{2}{8} = \dfrac{1}{4}$ _____

b. $\dfrac{8}{10} = \dfrac{4}{5}$ _____

c. $\dfrac{5}{8} = \dfrac{10}{12}$ _____

d. $\dfrac{2}{3} > \dfrac{3}{4}$ _____

e. $\dfrac{5}{8} < \dfrac{3}{4}$ _____

f. $\dfrac{1}{4} < \dfrac{6}{12}$ _____

❻ Taz had $60 in spending money this month. Calculate the fraction of $60 he spent on each item, and then reduce it to its simplest form.

	Item	Amount	Fraction	Simplest Form
a.	movies	$12		
b.	food/drink	$15		
c.	bus fares	$9		
d.	books	$10		
e.	go-karts	$14		

1 Write an improper fraction and a mixed number for the shaded part of each diagram.

a. _____ , _____

b. _____ , _____

e. _____ , _____

c. _____ , _____

d. _____ , _____

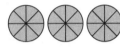

f. _____ , _____

2 Write the mixed number for the following.

a. $\frac{9}{5}$ _____

b. $\frac{8}{3}$ _____

c. $\frac{5}{2}$ _____

d. $\frac{8}{5}$ _____

e. $\frac{4}{3}$ _____

f. $\frac{10}{6}$ _____

3 Write the improper fraction for the following.

a. $2\frac{1}{2}$ _____

b. $1\frac{2}{5}$ _____

c. $2\frac{1}{3}$ _____

d. $4\frac{3}{5}$ _____

e. $2\frac{5}{8}$ _____

f. $4\frac{2}{5}$ _____

4 Write the mixed number for the following.

a. $\frac{15}{8}$ _____

b. $\frac{21}{10}$ _____

c. $\frac{11}{3}$ _____

d. $\frac{17}{10}$ _____

e. $\frac{15}{6}$ _____

f. $\frac{19}{5}$ _____

5 In the space below, draw a diagram to represent the following.

a. $\frac{6}{4}$

b. $4\frac{2}{3}$

6 $\boxed{2\frac{3}{4}, \ \frac{16}{4}, \ \frac{1}{4}, \ \frac{14}{4}, \ 3, \ \frac{10}{4}}$

a. Rewrite the values in the box above so that they are all fractions or improper fractions with the same denominator.

_____

b. Order the values in the box above from least to greatest.

_____

Using Fractions

1 Write *true* or *false* for each of the following.

a. $\frac{4}{3} < \frac{5}{6}$ _____

b. $\frac{11}{12} < \frac{5}{6}$ _____

c. $\frac{3}{6} < \frac{2}{3}$ _____

d. $\frac{7}{10} > \frac{3}{5}$ _____

e. $\frac{9}{10} > \frac{4}{5}$ _____

f. $\frac{5}{6} > \frac{2}{3}$ _____

2 Add the fractions. Use the strategy from the first two to solve the rest.

a. $\frac{2}{5} + \frac{1}{10} =$

$\frac{\square}{10} + \frac{\square}{10} =$ _____

b. $\frac{3}{4} + \frac{3}{8} =$

$\frac{\square}{8} + \frac{\square}{8} =$ _____

c. $\frac{1}{2} + \frac{3}{10} =$ _____

d. $\frac{1}{6} + \frac{2}{3} =$ _____

e. $\frac{3}{5} + \frac{3}{10} =$ _____

f. $\frac{1}{4} + \frac{5}{8} =$ _____

3 Subtract the fractions. Use the strategy from the first two to solve the rest.

a. $\frac{5}{6} - \frac{1}{3} =$

$\frac{\square}{6} - \frac{\square}{6} =$ _____

b. $\frac{7}{10} - \frac{2}{5} =$

$\frac{\square}{10} - \frac{\square}{10} =$ _____

c. $\frac{7}{8} - \frac{1}{2} =$ _____

d. $\frac{6}{12} - \frac{1}{3} =$ _____

e. $\frac{3}{4} - \frac{1}{2} =$ _____

f. $\frac{1}{2} - \frac{1}{10} =$ _____

4 Multiply the following.

a. $2 \times \frac{3}{5} =$ _____

b. $4 \times \frac{1}{3} =$ _____

c. $2 \times \frac{5}{12} =$ _____

d. $3 \times \frac{6}{10} =$ _____

e. $5 \times \frac{3}{4} =$ _____

f. $4 \times \frac{3}{8} =$ _____

5 Order the following fractions from least to greatest.

| one-sixth | $\frac{4}{3}$ | two and one-third | $\frac{2}{6}$ | two-thirds | 1 |

_____

6 George ate $\frac{5}{8}$ of a medium pizza in one day. Charlie ate $\frac{1}{2}$ of a medium pizza in one day. Who ate more pizza? _____

Fraction Addition

1 Add the fractions. Simplify when possible.

a. $\frac{7}{12} + \frac{3}{12} =$ _____

b. $\frac{2}{9} + \frac{4}{9} =$ _____

c. $\frac{5}{8} + \frac{1}{8} =$ _____

d. $\frac{1}{4} + \frac{1}{4} =$ _____

e. $\frac{2}{5} + \frac{1}{5} =$ _____

f. $\frac{3}{10} + \frac{5}{10} =$ _____

2 Add the following fractions using the number line. Convert each answer to a mixed number. Simplify when possible.

a. $\frac{8}{10} + \frac{5}{10} =$ _____

b. $\frac{6}{10} + \frac{9}{10} =$ _____

c. $\frac{11}{10} + \frac{6}{10} =$ _____

d. $\frac{5}{10} + \frac{7}{10} =$ _____

e. $\frac{8}{10} + \frac{7}{10} =$ _____

f. $\frac{14}{10} + \frac{5}{10} =$ _____

3 Add the fractions and then covert each answer to a mixed number. Simplify when possible.

a. $\frac{3}{5} + \frac{4}{5} =$ _____ $=$ _____

b. $\frac{7}{8} + \frac{7}{8} =$ _____ $=$ _____

c. $\frac{3}{4} + \frac{3}{4} =$ _____ $=$ _____

d. $\frac{6}{10} + \frac{7}{10} + \frac{4}{10} =$ _____ $=$ _____

e. $\frac{3}{4} + \frac{3}{4} + \frac{1}{4} =$ _____ $=$ _____

f. $\frac{3}{5} + \frac{4}{5} + \frac{4}{5} =$ _____ $=$ _____

4 Rewrite the fractions with common denominators before adding. Simplify when possible.

a. $\frac{1}{4} + \frac{7}{12} =$ _____

b. $\frac{1}{2} + \frac{3}{10} =$ _____

c. $\frac{1}{6} + \frac{2}{3} =$ _____

d. $\frac{3}{10} + \frac{4}{5} =$ _____

e. $\frac{1}{2} + \frac{5}{6} =$ _____

f. $\frac{1}{3} + \frac{2}{9} =$ _____

5 Sam and Kimmy each got a chocolate bar from their mom. Sam ate $\frac{1}{8}$ of his chocolate bar. Kimmy ate $\frac{3}{4}$ of her chocolate bar. What fraction of the chocolate bars did they eat altogether?

_____

6 To follow the recipe, Li has to add $\frac{1}{4}$ of a cup of 3 different flours and $\frac{1}{2}$ a cup of sugar. How much total flour and sugar does Li add?

_____

Fraction Subtraction

❶ Reduce each fraction to its simplest form.

  a. $\dfrac{20}{30}$ _____   b. $\dfrac{8}{12}$ _____   c. $\dfrac{6}{8}$ _____

  d. $\dfrac{14}{16}$ _____   e. $\dfrac{2}{10}$ _____   f. $\dfrac{8}{24}$ _____

❷ Subtract the fractions.

  a. $\dfrac{8}{10} - \dfrac{5}{10} =$ _____   b. $\dfrac{11}{12} - \dfrac{9}{12} =$ _____   c. $\dfrac{3}{8} - \dfrac{1}{8} =$ _____

  d. $\dfrac{5}{6} - \dfrac{4}{6} =$ _____   e. $\dfrac{3}{4} - \dfrac{1}{4} =$ _____   f. $\dfrac{7}{9} - \dfrac{4}{9} =$ _____

❸ Subtract the fractions by first rewriting the fractions with common denominators.

  a. $\dfrac{9}{10} - \dfrac{2}{5} =$ _____   b. $\dfrac{7}{8} - \dfrac{1}{4} =$ _____

  c. $\dfrac{5}{6} - \dfrac{2}{3} =$ _____   d. $\dfrac{4}{5} - \dfrac{1}{10} =$ _____

  e. $\dfrac{7}{9} - \dfrac{1}{3} =$ _____   f. $\dfrac{5}{6} - \dfrac{3}{12} =$ _____

❹ Find the difference between the following fractions.

  a. $\dfrac{6}{10}$ and $\dfrac{2}{5}$ _____   b. $\dfrac{7}{12}$ and $\dfrac{3}{6}$ _____

  c. $\dfrac{2}{3}$ and $\dfrac{4}{9}$ _____   d. $\dfrac{8}{10}$ and $\dfrac{2}{5}$ _____

  e. $\dfrac{3}{8}$ and $\dfrac{1}{4}$ _____   f. $\dfrac{4}{6}$ and $\dfrac{1}{2}$ _____

❺ Josi's teacher asked her to reach into a bag and pick two pieces of paper. Each paper had a fraction. Josi was to find the difference between the two. The first fraction was $\dfrac{5}{8}$. The second fraction was $\dfrac{1}{2}$. What answer should Josi give her teacher?

_____

❻ Out of the 10 slices of birthday cake, 7 were left. If 3 people each took 1 slice and 1 person took $\dfrac{1}{5}$ of the cake, what fraction of the cake is now left? In the box, draw a diagram to help you.

_____

Fraction Addition and Subtraction

① Write the improper fraction for the following.

a. $1\frac{6}{10}$ _____

b. $2\frac{1}{4}$ _____

c. $3\frac{2}{3}$ _____

d. $4\frac{5}{8}$ _____

e. $7\frac{1}{2}$ _____

f. $2\frac{4}{5}$ _____

② Write the mixed number for the following.

a. $\frac{4}{3}$ _____

b. $\frac{7}{5}$ _____

c. $\frac{21}{10}$ _____

d. $\frac{8}{4}$ _____

e. $\frac{17}{8}$ _____

f. $\frac{14}{6}$ _____

③ Add the fractions.

a. $\frac{1}{4} + \frac{1}{2} =$ _____

b. $\frac{2}{3} + \frac{4}{6} =$ _____

c. $\frac{3}{8} + \frac{1}{4} =$ _____

d. $\frac{7}{10} + \frac{2}{5} =$ _____

e. $\frac{1}{9} + \frac{2}{3} =$ _____

f. $\frac{1}{3} + \frac{5}{12} =$ _____

④ Subtract the fractions.

a. $\frac{5}{8} - \frac{1}{4} =$ _____

b. $\frac{9}{10} - \frac{4}{5} =$ _____

c. $\frac{5}{6} - \frac{2}{3} =$ _____

d. $\frac{11}{12} - \frac{3}{4} =$ _____

e. $\frac{4}{5} - \frac{1}{2} =$ _____

f. $\frac{7}{9} - \frac{2}{3} =$ _____

⑤ Lisa has $\frac{3}{4}$ of an apple and $\frac{5}{8}$ of an orange. What is the total amount that Lisa has of the two pieces of fruit? _____

⑥ Write a subtraction word problem using the fractions $\frac{7}{8}$ and $\frac{1}{2}$. Then solve it.

_____

_____

Fraction Multiplication

❶ Find the missing numerators.

a. $\dfrac{\square}{2} = 4\dfrac{1}{2}$

b. $\dfrac{\square}{5} = 6\dfrac{2}{5}$

c. $\dfrac{\square}{4} = 1\dfrac{1}{4}$

d. $3\dfrac{5}{6} = \dfrac{\square}{6}$

e. $2\dfrac{5}{8} = \dfrac{\square}{8}$

f. $7\dfrac{3}{10} = \dfrac{\square}{10}$

❷ Use repeated addition to complete the table.

	Question	Repeated Addition	Fraction	Simplified Fraction
a.	$2 \times \dfrac{3}{4}$	$\dfrac{3}{4} + \dfrac{3}{4}$		
b.	$3 \times \dfrac{1}{4}$			
c.	$4 \times \dfrac{2}{3}$			
d.	$3 \times \dfrac{3}{5}$			
e.	$2 \times \dfrac{6}{8}$			
f.	$4 \times \dfrac{2}{10}$			

❸ a. Anton ate $\dfrac{1}{4}$ of the pizza, which cost \$24. What value did he eat? _____

b. Chris spent $\dfrac{1}{5}$ of his \$200 salary on food. How much did he spend? _____

c. Connie used $\dfrac{1}{3}$ of a piece of wood 4.5 ft. long. What length did she use? _____

d. The water tank holds 6,000 gallons. If $\dfrac{1}{2}$ had been removed, how much was left? _____

❹ Multiply the following.

a. $3 \times \dfrac{3}{8} = $ _____

b. $2 \times \dfrac{3}{10} = $ _____

c. $5 \times \dfrac{2}{5} = $ _____

d. $4 \times \dfrac{2}{3} = $ _____

e. $6 \times \dfrac{3}{4} = $ _____

f. $9 \times \dfrac{5}{6} = $ _____

❺ Multiply the fractions.

a. $\dfrac{2}{3} \times \dfrac{1}{4} = $ _____

b. $\dfrac{4}{5} \times \dfrac{5}{6} = $ _____

c. $\dfrac{5}{8} \times \dfrac{2}{5} = $ _____

d. $\dfrac{6}{8} \times \dfrac{1}{4} = $ _____

e. $\dfrac{3}{5} \times \dfrac{3}{4} = $ _____

f. $\dfrac{4}{10} \times \dfrac{2}{3} = $ _____

❻ Solve the following.

a. $\dfrac{1}{5} \times 60 - 4 = $ _____

b. $20 - \dfrac{1}{10} \times 20 = $ _____

c. $\dfrac{1}{3} \times 27 + 9 = $ _____

Decimal Place Value — Thousandths

1 Draw each number on the abacus.

a. 15.281   **b.** 32.605   **c.** 0.295

| H | T | O | . | Tth | Hth | THth |

2 Write the numerals for each of the following.

a. nine and six-tenths_____   **b.** nine and twenty-seven hundredths_____

c. nineteen and fourteen thousandths_____   **d.** ninety and fifty-two thousandths_____

e. ninety and two-thousandths_____   **f.** nineteen and twenty-hundredths_____

3 What is the value of the 7 in each of the following?

a. 5.37 _____   **b.** 9.207 _____

c. 7.015 _____   **d.** 17.916 _____

e. 2.075 _____   **f.** 3.74 _____

4 Write the decimal for each of the following.

a. $\frac{22}{100}$ _____   **b.** $\frac{19}{100}$ _____   **c.** $\frac{4}{10}$ _____

d. $\frac{236}{1,000}$ _____   **e.** $\frac{4}{100}$ _____   **f.** $\frac{143}{1,000}$ _____

5 Write the following decimals in words.

a. 4.603 _____

b. 7.008 _____

c. 11.52 _____

6 Write the decimal indicated by the arrow on the number line. _____

3.260   3.270

Decimal Addition

① Add the decimals.

a.	b.	c.
3.21	9.70	5.82
+4.63	+2.46	+7.95

d.	e.	f.
3.486	4.372	9.810
+7.219	+2.765	+6.243

② Add the decimals.

a.	b.	c.	d.
8.40	7.98	3.79	46.215
2.16	2.10	2.40	1.98
+3.85	+4.83	+8.70	+17.246

③ Find the cost of the following purchases.

 $15.35 $8.95 $98.15

 $83.95 $49.50 $67.55

a. the music CD and the basketball hoop _____   b. the book and the skateboard _____

c. the dress and the shoes _____   d. 4 music CDs _____

e. 1 book and 2 basketball hoops _____   f. 2 dresses and 1 skateboard _____

④ Find each total.

a.	b.	c.	d.
$ 17.29	$ 58.62	$326.45	$212.45
$ 21.75	$ 39.80	$ 19.65	$ 86.65
$146.52	$ 27.45	$ 21.30	$110.50
+$125.95	+$125.45	+$ 3.57	+$142.95

⑤ Joey bought a special scale that measures things to the thousandth of a pound. His thick dictionary weighed 2.285 pounds. His printer weighed 9.816 pounds. What is the total weight of the two objects? _____

⑥ Write a word problem that matches the below number sentence. Then solve it.

4.29 miles + 3.60 miles + 15 miles = _____

_____

_____

Decimal Subtraction

1 Subtract the decimals.

    a. 1.0 – 0.8 = _____   **b.** 2.0 – 0.9 = _____

    c. 1.16 – 0.14 = _____   **d.** 2.45 – 0.32 = _____

    e. 5.7 – 2.4 = _____   **f.** 7.5 – 2.63 = _____

2 Subtract the decimals.

a. 2.47	**b.** 6.95	**c.** 42.83
– 1.83	– 2.18	– 21.95

d. 4.768	**e.** 3.061	**f.** 5.876
– 2.193	– 0.539	– 2.417

3 Find the difference between the following amounts.

    a. $25.63 and $19.48 _____   **b.** $176.25 and $90.72 _____

    c. $430.90 and $275.17 _____   **d.** $402.40 and $165.82 _____

    e. $176.50 and $95 _____   **f.** $210 and $173.47 _____

4 Subtract the decimals.

a. 96.5	**b.** 2.63	**c.** 14.2
– 38.72	– 1.7	– 9.605

d. 21.43	**e.** 11.00	**f.** 102.3
– 16.756	– 2.43	– 98.651

5 Johnny bought 6.75 ft. of wire for his school project. After he was finished, there was 2.83 ft. left. How much wire did Johnny use?

_____

6 Write a word problem that matches the following number sentence. Then solve it.

    $16.30 – $12.49 = _____

_____

_____

Decimal Multiplication

① Multiply the following.

a.   4.61
  ×   3

b.   7.98
  ×   2

c.   2.44
  ×   8

d.   1.537
  ×   3

e.   6.215
  ×   2

f.   19.214
  ×   8

② Find the cost of the following food purchases.

 $2.75

 $4.26

 $2.05

$4.10

$4.39

a. 3 loaves of bread _____   b. 5 packages of cookies _____

c. 6 cartons of milk _____   d. 2 jars of jam and 1 wedge of cheese _____

e. 2 loaves of bread and 1 wedge of cheese _____

f. 1 carton of milk, 2 packages of cookies, and 2 jars of jam _____

③ Multiply the following.

a. $6.95
  ×   6

b. $7.27
  ×   3

c. $51.65
  ×   2

d. $11.45
  ×   8

e. $133.59
  ×   9

f. $321.65
  ×   4

④ What is the total length of the following?

a. 6 lengths of 1.26 ft. of wood _____   b. 3 lengths of 1.75 ft. of ribbon _____

c. 9 lengths of 8.25 ft. of tape _____   d. 5 lengths of 15.29 ft. of hose _____

e. 7 lengths of 37.85 ft. of string _____   f. 4 lengths of 12.63 ft. of steel _____

⑤ Cooper has his favorite cartoon on DVD. The running time for the cartoon is 19.25 minutes. Cooper has already watched it 9 times. How many total minutes has he spent watching this cartoon? _____

⑥ Which of the following represents the best value for the money? Circle it.

    1 gallon of milk for $2.50   or   1 half-gallon of milk for $1.60

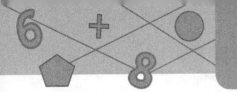

Decimal Division

① Divide the following.

    a. $2\overline{)6.86}$ **b.** $3\overline{)12.93}$ **c.** $4\overline{)25.6}$

    d. $7\overline{)64.47}$ **e.** $6\overline{)18.384}$ **f.** $8\overline{)34.728}$

② Divide the following.

    a. $2\overline{)16.2}$ **b.** $3\overline{)16.2}$ **c.** $4\overline{)16.2}$

    d. $5\overline{)16.2}$ **e.** $6\overline{)16.2}$ **f.** $9\overline{)16.2}$

③ Rounding to the nearest penny, find the cost per book if each set costs:

    a. $92.75 for 10 books. _____   **b.** $42.68 for 8 books. _____

    c. $22.50 for 2 books. _____   **d.** $24.48 for 4 books. _____

    e. $84.77 for 7 books. _____   **f.** $21.69 for 3 books. _____

④ Rounding to the nearest penny, find the cost of:

    a. 1 bar of soap if 5 cost $6.15. _____   **b.** 1 toilet paper roll if 8 cost $6.98. _____

    c. 1 bag of chips if 3 cost $2.00. _____   **d.** 1 box of crackers if 4 cost $3.00. _____

    e. 1 juice box if 6 cost $4.65. _____   **f.** 1 can of soda if 12 cost $3.96. _____

⑤ Divide the following.

    a. $45.36 \div 9 =$ _____   **b.** $16.2 \div 8 =$ _____

    c. $\$65.35 \div 5 =$ _____   **d.** $\$3.12 \div 4 =$ _____

⑥ Is the answer to the below division problem correct? If not, find the correct answer.

$$\begin{array}{r} 14.48 \\ 8\overline{)99.92} \end{array}$$

_____

Multiplication and Division of Decimals

1 Multiply the following decimals by 10.

a. 0.436 × 10 = _____

b. 2.176 × 10 = _____

c. 6.173 × 10 = _____

d. 0.9 × 10 = _____

e. 46.35 × 10 = _____

f. 0.071 × 10 = _____

2 Multiply the following decimals by 100 or 1,000.

a. 6.31 × 100 = _____

b. 0.472 × 100 = _____

c. 81.79 × 100 = _____

d. 6.421 × 1,000 = _____

e. 110.421 × 1,000 = _____

f. 26.5 × 1,000 = _____

3 Divide the following decimals by 10.

a. 0.452 ÷ 10 = _____

b. 6.71 ÷ 10 = _____

c. 12.96 ÷ 10 = _____

d. 130.21 ÷ 10 = _____

e. 421.639 ÷ 10 = _____

f. 214.853 ÷ 10 = _____

4 Divide the following decimals by 100 or 1,000.

a. 0.421 ÷ 100 = _____

b. 697.3 ÷ 100 = _____

c. 4.91 ÷ 100 = _____

d. 321.01 ÷ 1,000 = _____

e. 1,049.85 ÷ 1,000 = _____

f. 24.691 ÷ 1,000 = _____

5 Complete the table.

	× 1,000	× 100	× 10	Number	÷ 10	÷ 100
a.				46.83		
b.				924.10		
c.				4.63		
d.				10.48		
e.				110.216		
f.				30.05		

6 Write the following rules for multiplying and dividing decimals.

a. multiplying by 10: _____

b. multiplying by 100: _____

c. multiplying by 1,000: _____

d. dividing by 10: _____

e. dividing by 100: _____

Review of Decimal Operations

❶ Add the decimals.

  a.   7.3
       8.62
     +9.80

  b.   4.76
       1.02
     +3.4

  c.   8.92
      14.65
    + 1.2

  d. 4.836
      1.205
   +9.87

  e.   4.6
      2.81
   +7.395

  f. 121.49
     14.687
  + 31.249

❷ Find the difference between the following amounts.

  a. $6.85 and $3.96 _____

  b. $21.85 and $17.58 _____

  c. $10.07 and $7.88 _____

  d. $42.55 and $39.66 _____

  e. $21.95 and $16.07 _____

  f. $121.73 and $99.62 _____

❸ What is the total weight of the fruit?

  a. 6 bags of apples at 3.2 lb. each _____

  b. 7 bags of oranges at 4.8 lb. each _____

  c. 2 bags of pears at 10.69 lb. each _____

  d. 5 boxes of plums at 0.25 lb. each _____

  e. 3 boxes of kiwi at 0.75 lb. each _____

  f. 8 boxes of limes at 26.75 lb. each _____

❹ Divide the following.

  a. $5\overline{)6.145}$

  b. $2\overline{)9.864}$

  c. $3\overline{)24.24}$

  d. $7\overline{)24.493}$

  e. $4\overline{)19.684}$

  f. $6\overline{)21.810}$

❺ Solve the following.

  a.   19.215
     163.980
   + 14.761

  b. $14.08
   −$ 8.56

  c.   7.83
   ×   4

  d. $8\overline{)61.324}$

❻ Solve the following: 4.28 ft. + (3 × 6.31 ft.) − 1.72 ft. = _____

Fractions and Decimals

1 Write the decimal for each of the following fractions.

   a. $\frac{63}{100}$ = _____   **b.** $\frac{246}{1,000}$ = _____   **c.** $\frac{8}{10}$ = _____

   d. $\frac{9}{100}$ = _____   **e.** $\frac{42}{1,000}$ = _____   **f.** $\frac{6}{10}$ = _____

2 Write the fraction for each of the following decimals.

   a. 0.2 = _____   **b.** 0.85 = _____   **c.** 0.326 = _____

   d. 0.04 = _____   **e.** 0.406 = _____   **f.** 0.001 = _____

3 Find the decimal for the following fractions.

   a. $\frac{1}{5}$ = _____   **b.** $\frac{1}{20}$ = _____   **c.** $\frac{3}{4}$ = _____

   d. $\frac{1}{8}$ = _____   **e.** $\frac{3}{5}$ = _____   **f.** $\frac{3}{8}$ = _____

4 Complete the table to show the fraction and decimal that represents the shaded part of the hundred square.

	Hundred Square	Fraction of 100	Decimal
a.			
b.			
c.			

	Hundred Square	Fraction of 100	Decimal
d.			
e.			
f.			

5 **a.** In a basketball game, the home team made 56 out of 100 shot attempts. Write the decimal that represents the home team's **missed** shot attempts. _____

   b. In a swimming race, the difference between the winning time and the second-place time was 0.123 seconds. Write this difference as a fraction. _____

6 Shade the hundred square to show $\frac{6}{10}$.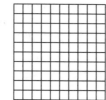

Rounding Decimals

❶ Round each of the following decimals to one decimal place (tenths place).

a. 6.23 _____   **b.** 4.69 _____   **c.** 1.08 _____

d. 143.461 _____   **e.** 28.012 _____   **f.** 17.965 _____

❷ Round each of the following decimals to two decimal places (hundredths place).

a. 6.493 _____   **b.** 8.021 _____   **c.** 7.395 _____

d. 211.0873 _____   **e.** 42.1197 _____   **f.** 879.6382 _____

❸ Round each of the following to the nearest whole number and then estimate the sum.

a. 10.045 + 2.673 + 105.95 _____

b. 2.216 + 3.63 + 19.04 _____

c. 902.5 + 18.699 + 15.02 _____

d. 7.041 + 8.92 + 3.856 _____

e. 421.02 + 1.03 + 4.71 _____

f. 12.58 + 2.6 + 19.058 _____

❹ Add or subtract the following decimals. Round each answer to the tenths place.

a. $\quad 0.463$
$\quad\quad 7.21$
$\quad +9.805$

b. $\quad 16.248$
$\quad\quad\; 1.119$
$\quad +32.6$

c. $\quad 42.809$
$\quad\quad 10.7$
$\quad +46.37$

d. $\quad 241.82$
$\quad -\;\; 97.63$

e. $\quad 827.106$
$\quad -413.942$

f. $\quad 780.29$
$\quad -356.025$

❺ **a.** Elsie wanted to see if she had enough money to buy the groceries listed below. Round each amount to the nearest dollar to estimate the total cost.

Juice $4.48	
Bread $2.95	
Milk $3.56	
Butter $3.27	
Jam $3.79	

Estimate = _____

b. If Elsie has $17, will she have enough to buy all of the items listed? _____

❻ Eric and Jeff bought a package of 12 pencils to share for $3.85, including tax. If they are splitting the cost, how much will each person pay? Round your answer to the nearest penny.

_____

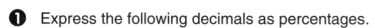

1 Express the following decimals as percentages.

a. 0.2 _____   **b.** 0.9 _____   **c.** 0.6 _____

d. 0.81 _____   **e.** 0.36 _____   **f.** 0.02 _____

2 Complete the table.

	a.	b.	c.	d.	e.	f.
Fraction	$\frac{3}{10}$	$\frac{9}{10}$	$\frac{41}{100}$	$\frac{73}{100}$	$\frac{27}{100}$	$\frac{14}{100}$
Decimal						
Percentage						

3 Circle the greatest value in each group.

a. $\frac{6}{10}$ 0.59 61%   **b.** 26% $\frac{25}{100}$ 0.24   **c.** 0.4 39% $\frac{41}{100}$

d. 0.89 90% $\frac{75}{100}$ **e.** 50% 0.45 $\frac{49}{100}$ **f.** $\frac{75}{100}$ 0.77 72%

4 Draw lines to match the equal percentages and fractions.

a. $\frac{1}{2}$ 10%

b. $\frac{1}{4}$ 5%

c. $\frac{1}{20}$ 75%

d. $\frac{1}{5}$ 20%

e. $\frac{3}{4}$ 50%

f. $\frac{1}{10}$ 25%

5 Shade each of the following shapes the given percentage, and then state the answers.

a.   **b.**   **c.**   **d.**

120   500   360   1,000

25% = _____   25% = _____   50% = _____   20% = _____

6 Complete the table to find out how much the discount and final price would be for the following items.

	a.	b.	c.	d.	e.	f.
Price	$20	$50	$30	$80	$900	$120
% Off	10%	50%	20%	25%	5%	20%
Discount						
Final Price						

Fractions, Decimals, and Percentages

❶ Express each of the following decimals as percentages.

a. 0.3 _____

b. 0.7 _____

c. 0.01 _____

d. 0.12 _____

e. 0.56 _____

f. 1.3 _____

❷ Express each of the following percentages as decimals.

a. 7% _____

b. 3% _____

c. 40% _____

d. 59% _____

e. 63% _____

f. 121% _____

❸ Express each of the following fractions as percentages.

a. $\frac{4}{10}$ _____

b. $\frac{8}{10}$ _____

c. $\frac{8}{100}$ _____

d. $\frac{90}{100}$ _____

e. $\frac{47}{100}$ _____

f. $\frac{136}{100}$ _____

❹ Circle the largest value in each group.

a. $\frac{89}{100}$ 0.85   87%

b. 0.33 $\frac{3}{10}$ 34%

c. $\frac{5}{100}$ 0.5   15%

❺ Circle the smallest value in each group.

a. 98%   0.99 $\frac{100}{100}$

b. 1.21 $\frac{120}{100}$ 123%

c. 7.6   750% $\frac{759}{100}$

❻ Express each percentage as a fraction in its simplest form.

a. 20% _____

b. 16% _____

c. 140% _____

d. 290% _____

Money in Shopping

1 List the fewest number of bills and coins needed to make the following amounts.

    a. $11.80 _____

    b. $27.15 _____

    c. $43.95 _____

    d. $126.45 _____

2 How much change would be received from $40 after spending the following amounts?

    a. $23.40 _____   **b.** $17.85 _____

    c. $34.15 _____   **d.** $11.90 _____

    e. $7.05 _____   **f.** $26.80 _____

3 **a.** If 1 tube of toothpaste costs $1.75, how much do 4 tubes cost? _____

    b. If 3 cans of corn cost $4.85, how much are 12 cans? _____

4 Find the total of each amount, then round to the nearest 5 cents.

a.	**b.**	**c.**	**d.**
$2.35	$11.25	$5.88	$4.77
$1.07	$6.37	$6.29	$2.98
$4.98	$4.21	$3.45	$1.06
+$6.62	+$3.02	+$1.06	+$3.48

5 **a.** What was the total cost of 2 loaves of bread at
    $2.95 each, 1 tub of margarine at $1.75, and
    1 jar of jam at $4.15?   _____

    b. Could Albert buy 2 magazines at $8.95 each
    and 2 chocolate bars at $1.20 each for $20?   _____

6 **a.** Which is better value? Circle it.

    5 oranges for $1.00   or   a bag of 15 oranges for $2.55

    b. If Joe bought 3 bottles of juice for $4.35 each, how
    much change did he receive from $20?   _____

Symmetry

1 How many lines of symmetry do each of the following shapes have?

a.  _____

b.  _____

c.  _____

d. _____

e.  _____

f. _____

2 Draw all the lines of symmetry for each of the following shapes.

a.

b.

c.

d.

e.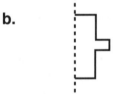

f.

3 Complete each of the following shapes by using the lines of symmetry.

a.

b.

c.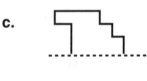

d.

e.

f.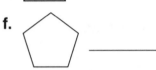

4 In the space below, draw shapes as indicated.

a. 5-sided symmetrical shape

b. 5-sided non-symmetrical shape

5 List all the capital letters that are symmetrical.

_____

6 Complete the picture so that it is symmetrical.

1 *Rotational symmetry* is when the tracing of a shape matches, after the shape is rotated (at the center) a **part** of a full turn. Do each of the following shapes have rotational symmetry? Write *yes* or *no*.

a. ☐ ____

b. ▽ ____

c. ◁ ____

d. ◯ ____

e. ⌂ ____

f. ⬡ ____

2 How many times can each of the following shapes be rotated within the same revolution to match the original shape? For example, a square can be rotated 4 times in one revolution and match its original position.

a. △ ____

b. ▭ ____

c. ▱ ____

d. ⬠ ____

e. ⬡ ____

f. ⬡ ____

3 Do each of the following have rotational symmetry? Write *yes* or *no*.

a. ____

b. ✦ ____

c. ↖ ____

d. ____

e. ____

f. ____

4 Draw the following shapes, after each has been rotated 90° clockwise around the marked point.

a. ◇

b. ⋁

c. ⇨

d. ▽

e. ◁

f. •——•

5 Draw the shape after it has been rotated 180° clockwise around the marked point.

6 Does this shape have rotational symmetry? If so, how many times can it be rotated to match the original shape?

_____

Diagonals, Parallel, and Perpendicular Lines

1 Circle the perpendicular lines.

a.

b.

c.

d.

e.

f.

2 Write *true* or *false* for each of the following statements about the diagram.

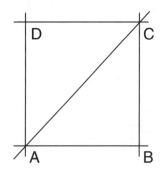

a. Lines AD and CD are perpendicular. _____

b. Lines AB and CD are perpendicular. _____

c. Lines BC and AD are parallel. _____

d. Lines AB and BC are at right angles. _____

e. Line CD is a diagonal. _____

f. Line AC is a diagonal. _____

3 Draw the diagonals on each of the following shapes.

a.

b.

c.

d.

e.

f.

4 Complete the table.

	Shape	Number of Sides	Number of Diagonals
a.	square		
b.	rectangle		
c.	pentagon		
d.	hexagon		
e.	heptagon		
f.	octagon		

5 Of the numbers 0 to 10, which contain perpendicular lines? _____

6 List all the capital letters that contain perpendicular lines. _____

Parallel, Horizontal, and Vertical Lines

1 Circle the parallel lines.

a.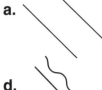

b.

c.

d.

e.

f.

2 Label the following as *vertical*, *horizontal*, or *neither*.

a. _____

b. 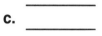 _____

c. _____

d. _____

e. _____

f. _____

3 Answer *true* or *false* for each of the statements about the diagram.

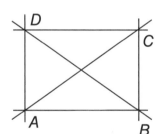

a. Line AC is a diagonal. _____

b. Line DC is vertical. _____

c. Lines AB and CD are parallel. _____

d. Lines AC and BD are parallel. _____

e. Lines AD and AB are perpendicular. _____

f. Lines AD and BC are horizontal. _____

4 Circle the following letters that have parallel lines.

a. A   b. H   c. E   d. F   e. N   f. G

5 List all of the capital letters that do not have any parallel, horizontal, or vertical lines.

_____

6 Draw diagrams of the following regular shapes to find which contains parallel lines.

Circle that shape.   **a.** pentagon   **b.** hexagon

Angles

❶ Give each angle measurement to the nearest degree.

a. 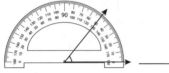 _____

b. 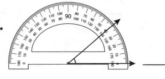 _____

c. 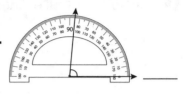 _____

d.  _____

e. 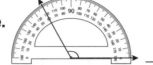 _____

f. 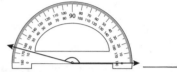 _____

❷ Use a protractor to measure each of the following to the nearest degree.

a.  _____

b.  _____

c.  _____

d. _____

e.  _____

f.  _____

❸ Circle the acute angles.

a. **b.** **c.**  **d.** **e.** 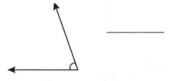 **f.**

❹ Circle the obtuse angles.

a. **b.** **c.** 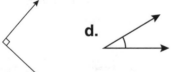 **d.** 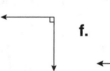 **e.** ... **f.** ...

❺ Circle the right angles.

a. **b.** **c.** **d.** **e.** **f.**

❻ Measure with a protractor to find the smallest angle between the clock hands. _____

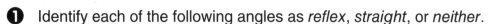

Reading Angles

1 Identify each of the following angles as *reflex*, *straight*, or *neither*.

a.  _____

b.  _____

c.  _____

d.  _____

e.  _____

f.  _____

2 Estimate the size of each of the following angles.

a.  _____

b.  _____

c.  _____

d.  _____

e.  _____

f.  _____

3 Name each of the following angle types.

a.  _____

b.  _____

c.  _____

d.  _____

e.  _____

f.  _____

4 Estimate the size of each angle before measuring it accurately with a protractor.

a. _____

b. _____

c. _____

d. _____

e. _____

f. _____

5 Find the size of each reflex angle by measuring the smaller angle first.

a.

b.

c.

d.

_____   _____   _____   _____

6 Measure with a protractor each of the angles of a pentagon. What did you discover?

 _____

Drawing Angles

① Draw each of the following angles using the starting lines.

a. 50°   **b.** 85°   **c.** 115°   **d.** 135°

② Draw the following in the space below.

a. an acute angle   **b.** an obtuse angle   **c.** a straight angle

d. a revolution   **e.** a reflex angle < 270°   **f.** a reflex angle > 270°

③ Use a protractor to draw angles of the following measurements.

a. 15°   **b.** 100°   **c.** 60°

④ Use a protractor to draw reflex angles of the following measurements.

a. 310°   **b.** 275°   **c.** 190°

⑤ In the box below, draw a triangle that has sides of different lengths. Then measure its interior angles and mark them on the line.

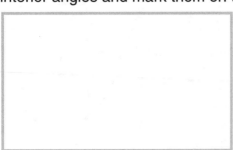

⑥ Using a protractor, draw a regular pentagon as accurately as possible in the space to the right.

Triangles

Triangle 1

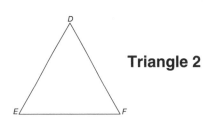

Triangle 2

❶ For triangle 1, measure the following angles.

a. A_____   **b.** B_____   **c.** C_____

For triangle 2, measure the following angles.

d. D_____   **e.** E_____   **f.** F_____

❷ For the triangles in question 1, name the angle type (*acute*, *obtuse*, or *right*) for the following angles.

a. A _____   **b.** B _____

c. C _____   **d.** D _____

Find the sum of angles:

e. A, B, C _____   **f.** D, E, F _____

❸ Find the missing angle in each of the following triangles.

a. 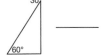 _____   **b.** 60° 60° _____   **c.** 130° 20° _____

d. 30° 100° _____   **e.** 70° 70° _____   **f.** 90° 45° _____

❹ Name the triangle type (*equilateral*, *isosceles*, *scalene*, or *right*) for each of the following.

a. _____   **b.** _____   **c.** _____

d. _____   **e.** _____   **f.** _____

❺ True or false?

a. A triangle can have angle measurements of 75°, 25°, and 85°. _____

b. A scalene triangle has no sides equal and no angles equal._____

❻ Draw a scalene triangle as accurately as possible with angles 10° and 20°.

3D Objects

❶ Name each object. Use the shape names in the box to help you.

> triangular prism   rectangular prism   triangular pyramid   cube
> pentagonal prism   hexagonal pyramid

a.  _____

b. _____

c. _____

d. _____

e. _____

f. _____

❷ Name each of the following solids.

a. _____

b. _____

c. _____

d. _____

e. _____

f. _____

❸ A *cross section* is the face that is seen when a 3D object is cut through. Match each of the cross sections below with the solids listed above in question 1.

a. _____   **b.** _____   **c.** _____

d. _____   **e.** _____   **f.** _____

❹ Complete the table.

	Object	Faces	Edges	Vertices
a.	cube			
b.	rectangular prism			
c.	triangular prism			
d.	hexagonal prism			
e.	square pyramid			
f.	triangular pyramid			

❺ Which 3D object can be made using the following faces?

 _____

❻ What am I? I have 5 vertices, 5 faces, and 8 edges.
I am made from 4 equilateral triangles and a square. _____

Drawing 3D Objects

1 List the shapes (number and type) that make up a:

    a. rectangular prism. _____

    b. square pyramid. _____

    c. cube. _____

    d. rectangular pyramid. _____

    e. triangular prism. _____

    f. hexagonal prism. _____

2 Place dotted lines in each of the following to provide the hidden detail.

    a. 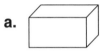   **b.**   **c.**

    d.   **e.**   **f.**

3 Look at each of the below objects and practice drawing them in the space beside each one.

    a.   **b.**   **c.**

    d.   **e.**   **f.**

4 Name the 3D objects that are constructed from the following shapes.

    a. 2 octagons and 8 rectangles _____

    b. 4 triangles _____

    c. 2 squares and 4 rectangles _____

    d. 1 hexagon and 6 triangles _____

5 Name a solid that has:

    a. less than 8 faces. _____   **b.** an even number of vertices. _____

6 In the box to the right, draw a 3D object that is constructed from 2 triangles and 3 rectangles.

Properties and Views of 3D Objects

❶ Complete the table.

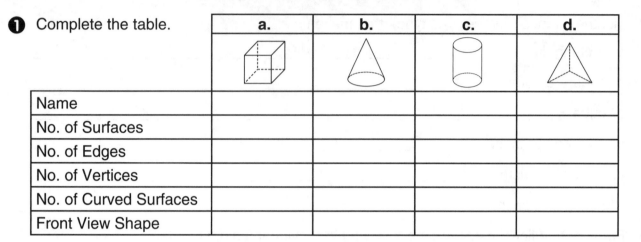

	a.	b.	c.	d.
Name				
No. of Surfaces				
No. of Edges				
No. of Vertices				
No. of Curved Surfaces				
Front View Shape				

❷ Which of the shapes in question 1 could have a view of:

a. ◯ _____

b. ⊙ _____

c. ▭ _____

d. △ _____

e. ▢ _____

f. ◁ _____

❸ Write the name of the container used in each stack.

a. _____

b. _____

c. _____

d. _____

❹ Write how many containers have been placed in each of the stacks in question 3.

a. _____   b. _____   c. _____   d. _____

❺ Circle the object that would be easier to stack.

triangular pyramid   or   triangular prism

❻ Name a real-life object that is in the shape of the following.

a. cube _____

b. rectangular prism _____

c. cylinder _____

d. triangular prism _____

Cylinders, Spheres, and Cones

1 Name each of the following objects.

a. _____   b. _____   c. _____

d. _____   e. _____   f. _____

2 Complete the table.

	a. Cone	b. Cylinder	c. Sphere	d. Cube
Side View Shape				
No. of Edges				
No. of Surfaces				
No. of Vertices				
No. of Curved Surfaces				
Does it roll?				

3 Of the objects in question 1:

a. Which object rolls the best? _____   b. How does a cone roll? _____

c. How does a cylinder roll? _____   d. Which object has no sides? _____

e. Which object meets at a point? _____

f. Which objects have one curved surface? _____

4 In the space below, sketch the following as described.

a. a cone on top of a cylinder   b. a sphere on top of a cone

5 For each real-life object below, give the name of the 3D shape it most closely resembles.

a. marble _____   b. peanut butter jar _____

c. marker _____   d. funnel _____

e. Earth _____   f. birthday party hat _____

6 Is it easier to stack spheres, cones, or cylinders? Draw a diagram in the box at the right to illustrate your answer.

_____

Nets and 3D Objects

❶ Complete the following table.

	Shape	Diagram	No. of Edges	No. of Vertices	No. of Surfaces
a.	cube				
b.	cylinder				
c.	cone				

	Shape	Diagram	No. of Edges	No. of Vertices	No. of Surfaces
d.	sphere				
e.	triangular prism				
f.	rectangular prism				

❷ Draw the top view of the following shapes:

a. cube

b. cylinder

c. cone

d. sphere

e. triangular pyramid

f. rectangular prism

❸ Name the 3D object that each net makes.

a.  _____

b. _____

c. 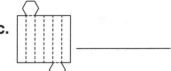 _____

d. _____

e. 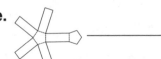 _____

f.  _____

❹ Circle the nets that make up an open cube. (Hint: Think of a box with no lid.)

a.

b.

c.

d.

e.

f.

❺ Name the 3D object that can be made using 6 rectangles and 2 octagons. _____

❻ Draw the net of a cylinder.

Parallelograms and Rhombuses

❶ Match the names and diagrams.

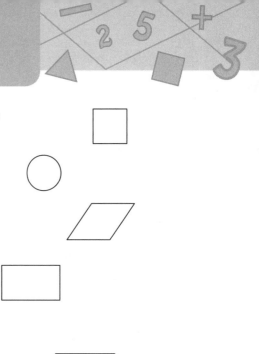

 a. square

 b. rhombus

 c. circle

 d. kite

 e. rectangle

 f. parallelogram

❷ Circle the shapes that are parallelograms.

 a.   **b.**   **c.**

 d.   **e.**   **f.**

❸ Circle the shapes that are rhombuses.

 a.   **b.**   **c.**

 d.   **e.**   **f.**

❹ Complete each of the parallelograms.

 a.   **b.**   **c.**   **d.**

❺ Is the below shape a parallelogram, rhombus, or trapezoid?

_____

❻ In the box at the right, draw a tessellating pattern (repeating without gaps or overlaps) using a rhombus.

Geometric Patterns

1 Complete the following table.

No. of Triangles	1	2	3	4	5	6	7
No. of Sides	3	a.	b.	c.	d.	e.	f.

2 Complete the following table.

No. of Pentagons	1	2	3	4	5	6	7
No. of Sides	a.	b.	15	c.	d.	e.	f.

3 Complete the following table.

No. of Octagons	1	2	3	4	5	6	7
No. of Sides	a.	b.	c.	d.	40	e.	f.

4 Repeat the following patterns.

a. △, △ ◯, ◯ ▢, ▢, _____, _____, _____, _____, _____, _____

b. ⌞, ⌜, ⌝, _____, _____, _____

c. ◠, ◡, _____, _____, _____, _____

d. ◿, ◹, ◺, _____, _____, _____

5 Write the rule for the pattern in:

a. question 1: _____

b. question 2: _____

c. question 3: _____

6 Write a rule for the following shape pattern.

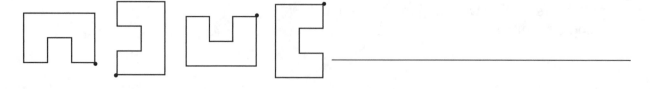

_____

Circles

1 Match the picture with its label.

a. center   **b.** radius   **c.** diameter   **d.** circumference   **e.** arc   **f.** sector

2 Match the label and description.

a. center   circles with a common center

b. semicircle   the perimeter of the circle

c. concentric circles   part of the circumference

d. circumference   the point in the middle

e. arc   half of the inside of the circle

f. sector   an area bound by two radii and an arc

3 Measure the diameter of each of the following circles in centimeters.

a. 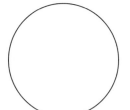 _____

b. _____

c. 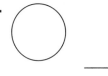 _____

d.  _____

e.  _____

f. _____

4 Measure the radius of each of the following circles in centimeters.

a.

b.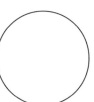

c.

d.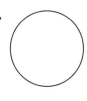

_____   _____   _____   _____

5 Describe a real-life object that represents the following.

a. center of circle _____

b. sector of circle _____

c. radius of circle _____

6 On another sheet of paper, draw a circle with a:

a. diameter of 2.5 inches   **b.** radius of 1 inch

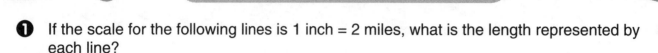

1 If the scale for the following lines is 1 inch = 2 miles, what is the length represented by each line?

a. _____ _____

b. _____ _____

c. _____ _____

d. _____ _____

2 If the scale for the following lines is 1 inch = 16 miles, what is the length represented by each line?

a. _____ _____

b. _____ _____

c. _____ _____

d. _____ _____

3 This ant has been drawn to a scale of 2:1 (it is 2 times larger than in real life). Use millimeters to measure the following.

What does this ant measure?

a. length of body _____

b. widest part of body _____

c. length of head _____

What does this ant measure in real life?

d. length of body _____

e. widest part of body _____

f. length of head _____

4 Complete the following table.

	Description	Length	Width	Scale	Scale Length	Scale Width
a.	backyard	50 ft.	30 ft.	1 in. = 5 ft.		
b.	field	200 ft.	150 ft.	1 in. = 20 ft.		
c.	pool	25 ft.	10 ft.	1 in. = 5 ft.		
d.	playground	900 ft.	500 ft.	1 in. = 100 ft.		
e.	park	7,500 ft.	4,500 ft.	1 in. = 500 ft.		
f.	rug	7 ft.	6 ft.	1 in. = 1 ft.		

5 If the scale is 1 ft.:12 mi., how long would a 6-inch river on a map be in real life? _____

6 Redraw the following triangle using a 1 cm: 1.5 cm scale.

Tessellation and Shape Movement

① A *tessellation* is a repeating pattern of one or more identical shapes that fit together without any gaps or overlaps. Will the following shapes tessellate? Write *yes* or *no*.

a.  ____   b.  ____   c. 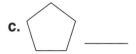 ____

d.  ____   e.  ____   f. ____

② Reflect (flip) each of the following shapes over the dotted line.

a.   b.    c.

d.    e.   f.

③ Translate (slide) each of the following shapes to the right.

a.   b.   c.

d.   e.   f.

④ Rotate (turn) each of the following shapes clockwise through 90° at the dot.

a.   b.   c.

d.   e.   f.

⑤ Create a tessellation in the box using only rectangles and triangles.

⑥ Draw a shape in the top-left box. Then rotate the small box clockwise at the black dot and draw what your shape looks like at each rotation.

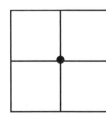

Compass Directions

1 What is the direction halfway between:

    a. north and east? _____   **b.** north and west? _____

    c. north and south? _____   **d.** south and east? _____

    e. south and west? _____   **f.** east and west? _____

2 If you are facing north, what direction is:

    a. to your left? _____   **b.** to your right? _____

    c. behind you? _____   **d.** in front of you? _____

    e. diagonally (45°) to your left? _____   **f.** diagonally (45°) to your right? _____

3 Using the grid, name the shape that is:

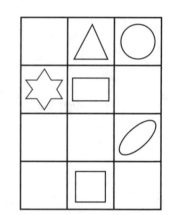

    a. east of the star. _____

    b. south of the rectangle. _____

    c. northeast of the rectangle. _____

    d. southwest of the oval. _____

    e. northwest of the oval. _____

    f. west of the circle. _____

4 Starting from the point X and using north as up, following each of the directions below, describe where you end up in relation to X.

    a. go 20 in. N, then 15 in. W, then 30 in. S

    _____

    b. go 10 in. E, then 8 in. S, then 8 in. W

    _____

    c. go 15 in. E, then 20 in. N, then 20 in. E, then 10 in. S

    _____

    d. go 12 in. S, then 5 in. E, then 6 in. N, then 5 in. W

    _____

5 Using the grid in question 3, write the directions (using north as up):

    a. for the star to get to the square. _____

    b. for the circle to get to the rectangle. _____

6 What angle measurement is formed between the following compass directions?

    a. south and west _____   **b.** north and east _____   **c.** east and west _____

Maps

1 Use the directions and distances to find each destination.

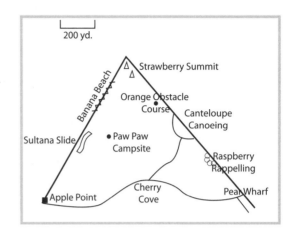

a. start at Paw Paw Campsite and travel north 200 yd. _____

b. then travel 200 yd. southwest _____

c. then travel 400 yd. south, then 200 yd. west _____

d. then travel east 600 yd. _____

e. then travel north 500 yd. _____

f. then travel northwest 100 yd. _____

2 Estimate the distance between each of the locations.

a. Raspberry Rappelling to Apple Point _____

b. Cherry Cove to Orange Obstacle Course _____

c. Apple Point to Strawberry Summit _____

d. Pear Wharf to Paw Paw Campsite _____

3 Give the direction of each of the following from Paw Paw Campsite.

a. Apple Point _____

b. Pear Wharf _____

c. Banana Beach _____

d. Sultana Slide _____

e. Cherry Cove _____

f. Raspberry Rappelling _____

4 Give the coordinates for the positions of the children marked on the map.

a. Yasu _____

b. Tom _____

c. Arthur _____

d. Amy _____

e. Jack _____

f. Li _____

Scale

150 ft.

5 Mark the following coordinates on the map.

a. C2   **b.** F3   **c.** I8   **d.** D6   **e.** G7   **f.** A6

6 Use the scale to calculate the shortest distance between the following locations.

a. Parking Lot and Office_____

b. Office and the Grades 3 & 4 building_____

c. Bridge and the Grade 6 building_____

d. Grade 5 building and Grade 6 building_____

e. Library and Office_____

f. Grade 6 building and the Parking Lot_____

Drawing a Map

1 Draw vertical lines and label them A–H. Use the marks that have been supplied.

2 Draw the horizontal lines and label them 0–7 to complete the coordinate grid.

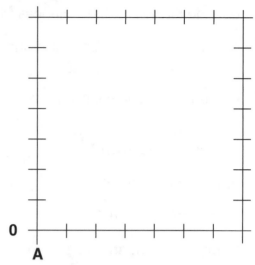

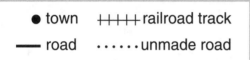

• town	┼┼┼┼┼ railroad track
— road	·····unmade road

3 Use the coordinate points to add the following towns on the map.

a. Green Town (B6) **b.** Blue Town (C2) **c.** Yellow Town (E4)

d. Orange Town (F3) **e.** Red Town (G5) **f.** Purple Town (D1)

4 Complete the paths on the map by drawing:

a. a road between Green Town and Red Town.

b. a railroad track between Blue Town and Purple Town.

c. an unmade road between Yellow Town and Orange Town.

d. a road between Blue Town and Red Town that runs through Yellow Town.

e. a railroad track between Orange Town and Purple Town that runs through Green Town.

f. an unmade road between Red Town and Purple town that runs through Orange Town.

5 **a.** Mark north on the map.

b. Add a lake at G1.

c. Add Black Town to the map at B1.

d. Draw a road between Black Town and Blue Town.

6 Give the compass direction from:

a. Black Town to Green Town. _____

b. Orange Town to Purple Town. _____

c. Purple Town to Blue Town. _____

Coordinates

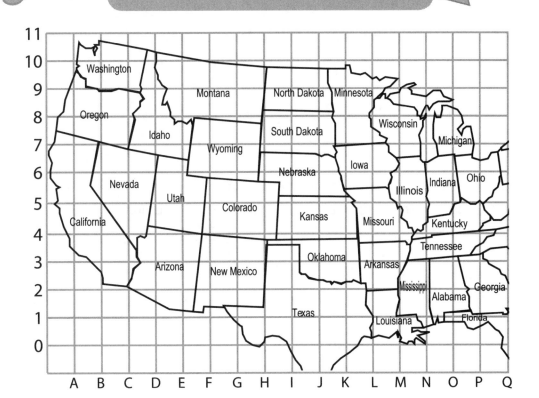

1 Name the state that is located at the following coordinates on the grid.

    a. J6 _____   **b.** G3 _____   **c.** C6 _____

2 Give the coordinates for the following states, where each state name mostly appears.

    a. Iowa _____   **b.** Oregon _____   **c.** Alabama _____

3 Give the main direction to:

    a. Utah from Arizona. _____   **b.** North Dakota from Montana. _____

    c. Arkansas from Louisiana. _____   **d.** Ohio from Kentucky. _____

4 Give the state that is:

    a. west of Idaho. _____   **b.** north of Illinois. _____

    c. east of Louisiana. _____   **d.** south of Kentucky. _____

5 Tell which state you would be in if you started at:

    a. J5 and traveled north 4 lines._____

    b. C9 and traveled east 8 lines. _____

    c. P6 and traveled south 4 lines. _____

6 On the back of this paper list the states that you would travel through, in order, if you left California and took the shortest route to Louisiana.

Analog Time

1 Draw each of the following times on the clock faces.

a. half past 9   **b.** 4 o'clock   **c.** 12 o'clock   **d.** half past 7   **e.** half past 11   **f.** 8 o'clock

2 Draw each of the following times on the clock faces.

a. quarter to 3   **b.** quarter past 5   **c.** quarter to 12   **d.** quarter past 2   **e.** quarter to 9   **f.** quarter past 8

  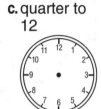 

3 Write each of the following times in words.

a. _____   **b.** _____   **c.** _____   **d.** _____

4 Find the difference between half past 1 and the time shown.

a. _____   **b.** _____   **c.** _____   **d.** _____

5 Lunchtime ends at 25 minutes past 1. If there is $1\frac{3}{4}$ hours left of school, what time will the bell ring to go home?   _____

6 Draw the times your school starts and ends on the clocks. Then calculate the total length of the school day.

Start   End   Total time = _____

Digital Time

1 Write each of the following in digital time.

a.  _____

b.  _____

c.  _____

d.  _____

e.  _____

f.  _____

2 For each of the following digital times, write *morning*, *afternoon*, or *evening*.

a.

_____

b.

_____

c.

_____

d.

_____

e.

_____

f.

_____

3 Write the time using *a.m.* or *p.m.*

a. 6:58 in the morning _____

b. 7:10 in the evening _____

c. 3:16 in the afternoon _____

d. 2:11 in the morning _____

e. 1:23 in the afternoon _____

f. 1:06 in the morning _____

4 Find the difference between:

a. 1:30 p.m. and 4:59 p.m. _____

b. 7:48 a.m. and 9:15 a.m. _____

c. 4:25 p.m. and 7:12 p.m. _____

d. 4:47 p.m. and 10:19 p.m. _____

e. 10:40 a.m. and 2:37 p.m. _____

f. 11:05 a.m. and 5:52 p.m. _____

5 Order the times from latest in the day to earliest.

a. 1:37 a.m., 12:00 p.m., 11:49 p.m. _____

b. 6:30 p.m., 6:31 a.m., 6:32 p.m. _____

c. 12:01 a.m., 10:25 p.m., 9:14 a.m. _____

6 Complete the clocks to show a difference in time of 6 hours and 26 minutes.

 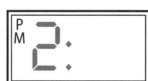

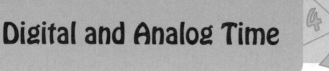

Digital and Analog Time

❶ Write each of the following times in words.

a. _____ **b.** _____ **c.** _____ **d.** _____

❷ Draw each of the following times on the clock faces.

a. 1:59 **b.** 8:26 **c.** 6:44 **d.** 5:09 **e.** 2:21 **f.** 4:40

❸ Write each of the following as a digital time.

a. _____ **b.** _____ **c.** _____ **d.** _____ **e.** _____ **f.** _____

❹ Write each of the following as a digital time.

a. quarter to 1 _____ **b.** 27 minutes past 4 _____

c. 42 minutes past 9 _____ **d.** 6 minutes to noon _____

e. quarter past 6 _____ **f.** 19 minutes to 5 _____

❺ Find the difference between the following times.

a. 10:35 a.m. and 2:47 p.m. _____

b. 1:23 p.m. and 7:59 p.m. _____

c. 8:04 p.m. and 6:16 a.m. _____

❻ What time is:

a. 38 minutes past 3:52 p.m.? _____

b. 2 hours and 11 minutes past 10:45 a.m.? _____

c. 3 hours and 24 minutes before 4:05 p.m.? _____

Stopwatches

1 What do each of these stopwatch times mean?

a. 06:24:14 _____

b. 13:36:40 _____

c. 00:06:29 _____

d. 01:43:05 _____

e. 25:13:19 _____

f. 47:12:63 _____

2 Circle the faster (shorter) time in each pair.

	Time 1	**Time 2**
a.	00:09:64	00:09:60
b.	03:26:71	03:30:85
c.	11:42:19	11:40:42

3 Circle the slower (longer) time in each pair.

	Time 1	**Time 2**
a.	35:25:40	34:37:56
b.	44:18:98	44:20:29
c.	26:25:40	26:35:10

4 Write the difference in time between the following.

a. 07:40:71 and 07:40:65 _____ **b.** 10:05:26 and 10:05:37 _____

c. 28:12:43 and 28:14:28 _____ **d.** 17:26:19 and 17:35:22 _____

e. 41:37:56 and 42:45:58 _____ **f.** 03:59:42 and 04:00:56 _____

5 Convert each of the following time facts.

a. $4\frac{1}{2}$ hours = _____ minutes   **b.** 75 minutes = _____ seconds

c. 360 seconds = _____ minutes   **d.** 35 days = _____ weeks

e. $2\frac{1}{2}$ days = _____ hours   **f.** $4\frac{1}{2}$ years = _____ weeks

6 Complete the table.

Days	Hours	Minutes	Seconds
$1\frac{1}{2}$			

Time Lines and Timetables

❶ Mark the beginning of each of the tropical cyclones on the time line.

a. Phoebe: August 31

b. Raymond: December 31

c. Sally: January 7

d. Tim: January 23

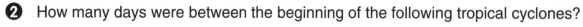

Aug.   Sep.   Oct.   Nov.   Dec.   Jan.   Feb.   Mar.   Apr.
          2004   **2005**

e. Vivienne: February 5

f. Ingrid: March 5

❷ How many days were between the beginning of the following tropical cyclones?

a. Sally and Tim _____   **b.** Vivienne and Ingrid _____   **c.** Raymond and Ingrid _____

❸ Design a time line to show the following events in Cooper's life.

a. went to camp 2006   **b.** born 1995   **c.** joined basketball team 2005

d. started school 2000   **e.** went to China 2003   **f.** broke arm 2002

❹ Color the timetable to show what time(s) the train leaves:

a. Budgie Station the first time. (red)

b. Duck Station the last time. (yellow)

c. Parrot Station in the morning. (blue)

d. Cocky Station in the morning. (green)

e. Swan Station in the afternoon. (pink)

f. Galah Station in the afternoon. (brown)

Monday to Friday Train Timetable					
Station	**a.m.**	**a.m.**	**p.m.**	**p.m.**	**p.m.**
Galah	10:55	11:20	12:00	12:55	1:20
Cocky	11:00	11:25	12:05	1:00	1:25
Parrot	11:07	11:32	12:12	1:07	1:32
Budgie	11:17	11:42	12:22	1:17	1:42
Swan	11:26	11:51	12:31	1:26	1:51
Duck	11:30	11:55	12:35	1:30	1:55

❺ Use the timetable to answer the following questions.

Los Angeles, CA, to Santa Fe, NM — Flight Timetable					
L.A. (departure)	8:30 a.m.	11:30 a.m.	2:30 p.m.	3:30 p.m.	6:30 p.m.
Santa Fe (arrival)	10:30 a.m.	1:30 p.m.	4:30 p.m.	5:30 p.m.	8:30 p.m.

How many flights leave Los Angeles: **a.** before noon? _____   **b.** after noon? _____

Give the arrival time in Santa Fe for the following Los Angeles departure times.

c. 3:30 p.m. _____   **d.** 8:30 a.m. _____   **e.** 6:30 p.m. _____   **f.** 11:30 a.m. _____

❻ **a.** Using the timetable in question 4, if the next train leaves Galah Station at 2:50 p.m., what time does it arrive at Swan Station? _____

b. On the timetable in question 5, how long is the flight? _____

Time Zones

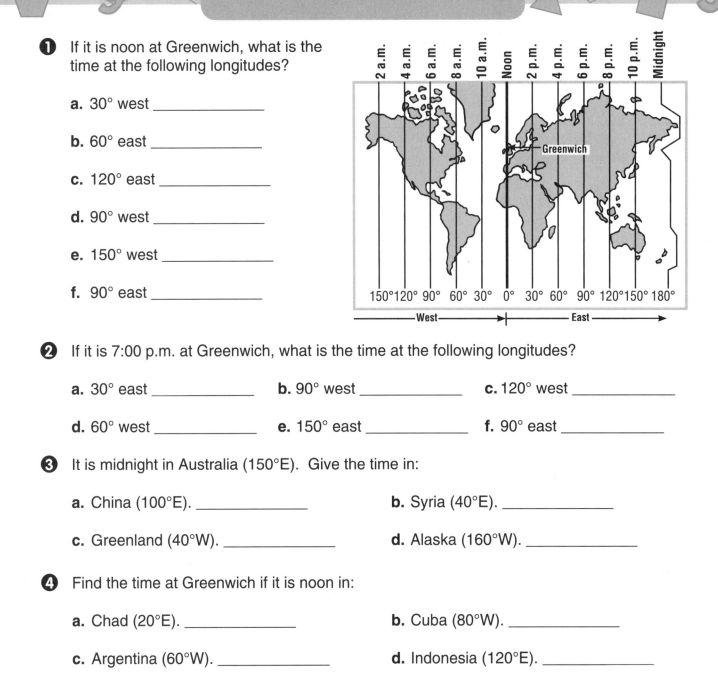

1 If it is noon at Greenwich, what is the time at the following longitudes?

    a. 30° west _____

    b. 60° east _____

    c. 120° east _____

    d. 90° west _____

    e. 150° west _____

    f. 90° east _____

2 If it is 7:00 p.m. at Greenwich, what is the time at the following longitudes?

    a. 30° east _____
    b. 90° west _____
    c. 120° west _____

    d. 60° west _____
    e. 150° east _____
    f. 90° east _____

3 It is midnight in Australia (150°E). Give the time in:

    a. China (100°E). _____
    b. Syria (40°E). _____

    c. Greenland (40°W). _____
    d. Alaska (160°W). _____

4 Find the time at Greenwich if it is noon in:

    a. Chad (20°E). _____
    b. Cuba (80°W). _____

    c. Argentina (60°W). _____
    d. Indonesia (120°E). _____

5 Make up your own question using the time zone chart. Then answer it.

_____

_____

6 **a.** Write the time it is where you are right now. _____

    b. If Greenwich is in a time zone that is 8 hours ahead of you, what time would it be in Greenwich? _____

Traveling Speed

1 Give each of the following as an average speed.

    a. 100 miles in 2 hours _____   **b.** 50 miles in 30 minutes _____

    c. 1,600 miles in 20 hours _____   **d.** 270 miles in 3 hours _____

    e. 130 miles in 2 hours _____   **f.** 180 miles in 4 hours _____

2 Give the distance traveled in:

    a. 7 hours at 80 mph. _____   **b.** 5 hours at 75 mph. _____

    c. $2\frac{1}{2}$ hours at 70 mph. _____   **d.** 20 minutes at 60 mph. _____

    e. 60 minutes at 70 mph. _____   **f.** 45 minutes at 88 mph. _____

3 Give the time taken to travel:

    a. 2 miles at 1 mph. _____   **b.** 250 miles at 100 mph. _____

    c. 900 miles at 90 mph. _____   **d.** 35 miles at 70 mph. _____

4 Complete the following table.

	Distance	Time	Average Speed
a.	30 miles	1 hour	
b.	100 miles		50 mph
c.	1 mile	10 minutes	
d.		3 hours	80 mph

5 A bus leaves at 6:15 a.m. and arrives at its destination at 3:45 p.m., 665 miles away. What was the average speed of the bus? _____

6 Josh rode his bike from his house to the library, which is half a mile away, at an average speed of 10 miles per hour. How long did it take Josh to get there? _____

Length in Inches, Feet, Yards, and Miles

1 Select the most suitable unit of measurement (in., ft., or mi.) for each of the following.

a. the length of a pencil _____   **b.** the width of a car _____

c. the length of a classroom _____   **d.** the height of a drink bottle _____

e. the distance from your home to the movie theater _____

f. the distance between your bedroom and the bathroom _____

2 Use decimal form to write each of the following in feet.

a. 6 in. _____   **b.** 24 in. _____

c. 18 in. _____   **d.** 42 in. _____

e. 21 in. _____   **f.** 15 in. _____

3 How many inches are there in the following lengths?

a. 2 ft. _____   **b.** 1 yd. _____

c. 1.5 ft. _____   **d.** 2.75 ft. _____

e. 2.5 ft. _____   **f.** 3 ft. _____

4 Use fractions to write each of the following in yards.

a. 3 ft. 12 in. _____   **b.** 5 ft. _____

c. 2 ft. _____   **d.** 9 in. _____

e. 18 in. _____   **f.** 2 ft. 3 in. _____

5 If a pool is 25 yards long, indicate how many laps of the pool will be swum in each of the following events.

a. 200 yd. freestyle _____   **b.** 100 yd. breaststroke _____

c. 500 yd. freestyle _____   **d.** 4 x 100 yd. relay _____

e. 100 yd. butterfly _____   **f.** 50 yd. freestyle _____

6 List five objects in the room that are approximately 1 yard long.

_____   _____

_____   _____

_____

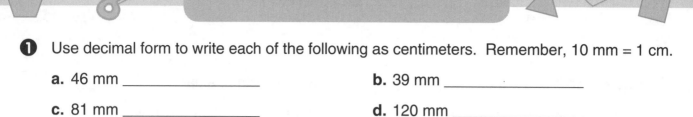

Converting Metric Lengths

1 Use decimal form to write each of the following as centimeters. Remember, 10 mm = 1 cm.

a. 46 mm _____

b. 39 mm _____

c. 81 mm _____

d. 120 mm _____

e. 146 mm _____

f. 276 mm _____

2 Use decimal form to write each of the following as meters. Remember, 100 cm = 1 m.

a. 461 cm _____

b. 738 cm _____

c. 926 cm _____

d. 1,284 cm _____

e. 3,695 cm _____

f. 2,100 cm _____

3 Complete the table. Remember, 1,000 m = 1 km.

	Meters	Kilometers
a.	1,376	
b.	4,218	
c.	5,798	
d.	6,635	
e.	9,801	
f.	10,635	

4 Complete each of the following conversions.

a. 55 m = _____ cm

b. 11.5 cm = _____ mm

c. 520 cm = _____ m

d. 9,240 m = _____ km

e. 4.7 km = _____ m

f. $2\frac{1}{2}$ cm = _____ mm

5 Complete the table.

	mm	cm	m
a.			0.6
b.	46		
c.		83	
d.			0.042
e.	19		
f.		24.1	

6 If the running track is 400 m long and Leah runs 12 laps each day, how far does she run in total in:

a. meters? _____

b. kilometers? _____

Perimeter

❶ Find the perimeter of each of the following shapes.

a.  _____

b.  _____

c. 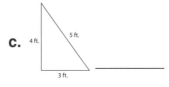 _____

d. _____

e.  _____

f. _____

❷ Shade the box with the correct perimeter for each of the following rectangles.

	Length	Width	Perimeter		
a.	4 in.	3 in.	12 in.	14 in.	16 in.
b.	9 cm	7 cm	32 cm	63 cm	36 cm
c.	11 ft.	9 ft.	40 ft.	44 ft.	99 ft.
d.	6 cm	3.5 cm	16 cm	18.5 cm	19 cm
e.	16 in.	4 in.	40 in.	64 in.	80 in.
f.	20 in.	15 in.	70 in.	150 in.	300 in.

❸ Complete the table.

	Shape	Side Length	Perimeter
a.	square	7.2 cm	
b.	equilateral triangle	19 ft.	
c.	regular pentagon	6 in.	
d.	regular hexagon	11 in.	
e.	regular octagon	14 ft.	
f.	regular decagon	12 cm	

❹ Find the perimeter of each of the following shapes.

a. 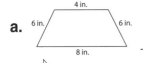 _____

b. 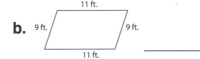 _____

c. 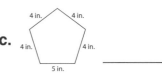 _____

d.  _____

e.  _____

f. 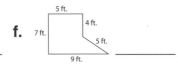 _____

❺ Find the side lengths of each of the squares with the following perimeters.

a. 20 cm _____

b. 16 in. _____

c. 64 ft. _____

d. 100 in. _____

e. 144 cm _____

f. 96 ft. _____

❻ a. On which polygons can we use shortcuts to find the perimeter? _____

b. Draw and label an example of an isosceles triangle with a perimeter of 40 inches. (Does not need to be to scale.)

Area of Squares and Rectangles

1 Complete the table.

	Diagram	Length (in.)	Width (in.)	Area (in.²)
a.	4 × 4			
b.	6 × 2			
c.	7 × 3			
d.	5 × 5			
e.	2 × 1			
f.	12 × 5			

2 Calculate the area of each of the following shapes.

a. 11 ft. × 9 ft. _____

b. 4 cm × 8 cm _____

c. 5 in. × 8 in. _____

d. 9 cm × 12 cm _____

e. 1.5 ft. × 1 ft. _____

f. 9 in. _____

3 Shade the box with the correct area for each of the following rectangles.

	Length (ft.)	Width (ft.)	Area (ft.²)		
a.	10	3	17	34	30
b.	5	8	13	26	40
c.	9	6	40	54	63
d.	4	2	8	16	20
e.	7	3	20	21	23
f.	11	9	40	81	99

4 Complete the following table.

	Length (cm)	Width (cm)	Area (cm²)
a.	4	3	
b.	9	2	
c.	15	10	
d.	20	4	
e.	100	50	
f.	60	3	

5 Find the area of each of the following shapes.

a. 7 in., 2 in., 3 in., 4 in. _____

b. 5 ft., 3 ft., 2 ft., 3 ft. _____

c. 2 in., 2 in., 3 in., 3 in., 4 in., 9 in. _____

6 Find two possible side lengths (using whole numbers only) of a rectangle that has an area of 42 in.².

_____

Area of Rectangles and Triangles

① Complete the following table by finding the area of each rectangle, and then dividing by 2 to find the area of one of its triangles.

	Diagram	Area of Rectangle (in.²)	Area of Triangle (in.²)
a.	5 in. × 4 in.		
b.	7 in. × 4 in.		
c.	8 in. × 3 in.		
d.	8 in. × 8 in.		
e.	10 in. × 9 in.		
f.	6 in. × 2 in.		

② Find the area of each of the shaded triangles.

a. 6 ft. / 7 ft. _____

b. 9 ft. / 4 ft. _____

c. 5 ft. / 12 ft. _____

d. 3 ft. / 4 ft. _____

e. 5 ft. / 10 ft. _____

f. 6 ft. _____

③ Complete the following table.

	Base (cm)	$\frac{1}{2}$ Base (cm)	Height (cm)	Area (cm²)
a.	6		3	
b.	4		7	
c.	8		9	
d.	10		6	
e.	12		10	
f.	20		4	

④ Find the area of each triangle.

a. 8 cm / 6 cm _____

b. 7 ft. / 7 ft. _____

c. 9 in. / 2 in. _____

d. 3 ft. / 10 ft. _____

e. 5 in. / 20 in. _____

f. 4 cm / 5 cm _____

⑤ Find the area of each of the following triangles with the given measurements.

a. $b = 6$ in. and $h = 9$ in. _____

b. $b = 4$ in. and $h = 8$ in. _____

c. $b = 20$ in. and $h = 10$ in. _____

d. $b = 4$ ft. and $h = 5$ ft. _____

e. $b = 12$ ft. and $h = 12$ ft. _____

f. $b = 20$ ft. and $h = 7$ ft. _____

⑥ Find the area of the trapezoid. Use what you know about area of rectangles and triangles to help you.

8 cm / 12 cm / 2 cm / 2 cm _____

Weight in Ounces, Pounds, and Tons

1 Select the most suitable unit of weight (ounces, pounds, or tons) for measuring each of the following. Remember, 16 oz. = 1 lb. and 2,000 lb. = 1 T.

a. a dog _____

b. a train _____

c. a man _____

d. a cup _____

e. a ship _____

f. a pen _____

2 Write the following weights to show pounds in decimal form.

a. 4 lb. 8 oz. _____

b. 8 lb. 4 oz. _____

c. 9 lb. 16 oz. _____

d. 5 lb. 12 oz. _____

e. 7 lb. _____

f. 3 lb. 16 oz. _____

3 How many ounces are there in each of the following weights?

a. 6 lb. _____

b. $5\frac{3}{4}$ lb. _____

c. $4\frac{1}{2}$ lb. _____

d. $2\frac{1}{4}$ lb. _____

e. $10\frac{3}{16}$ lb. _____

f. $11\frac{8}{16}$ lb. _____

4 Rewrite each of the following as pounds and ounces.

a. 116 oz. _____

b. 128 oz. _____

c. 152 oz. _____

d. 204 oz. _____

e. 165 oz. _____

f. 87 oz. _____

5 How many pounds are there in each of the following weights?

a. 2 T _____

b. 9 T _____

c. $4\frac{1}{2}$ T _____

d. $11\frac{3}{4}$ T _____

e. $15\frac{1}{4}$ T _____

f. $20\frac{7}{10}$ T _____

6 When fully loaded, the weight of the delivery truck is 4 T 390 lb. After the first delivery was dropped off, the weight of the truck became 2 T 760 lb. What was the weight of the first delivery?

_____

Volume

1 Select the most suitable unit (in.³ or ft.³) to find the volume of the following.

a. a shoe box _____

b. a briefcase _____

c. a garage _____

d. a refrigerator _____

e. a classroom _____

f. an ice cream container _____

2 What is the volume of each of the following in cubic units (units³)?

a. 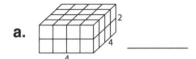 _____

b. 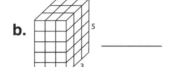 _____

c. 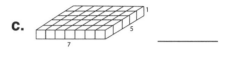 _____

d. 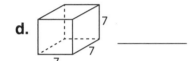 _____

e. 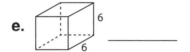 _____

f. 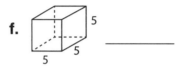 _____

3 Calculate the volume of each of the following prisms.

	Length (in.)	Width (in.)	Height (in.)	Volume (in.³)
a.	8	4	2	
b.	6	3	7	
c.	2	1	8	
d.	4	2	2	
e.	1	1	2	
f.	5	3	1	

4 Find the volume of each of the following shapes in cubic units.

a.  _____

b. 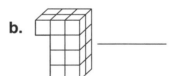 _____

c. 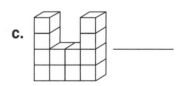 _____

5 Find the volume of each of the following prisms (measurements in inches).

a. 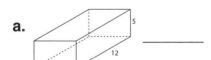 _____

b. 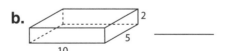 _____

c. 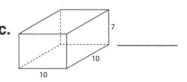 _____

6 Complete the table by finding 3 different prisms that each have a volume of 24 ft.³.
The first one has been started for you.

Volume (ft.³)	Length (ft.)	Width (ft.)	Height (ft.)
24	2	2	
24			
24			

Cubic Centimeters

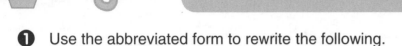

1 Use the abbreviated form to rewrite the following.

    a. 9 cubic centimeters _____   **b.** 14 cubic centimeters _____

    c. 32 cubic centimeters _____   **d.** 46 cubic centimeters _____

2 Complete the table.

	Diagram	Length (cm)	Width (cm)	Height (cm)	Volume (cm³)
a.	3 cm, 2 cm, 2 cm				
b.	2 cm, 1 cm, 4 cm				
c.	6 cm, 4 cm, 3 cm				
d.	2 cm, 4 cm, 5 cm				

3 Calculate the volume of each of the following prisms.

    a. 4 cm, 4 cm, 5 cm _____   **b.** 2 cm, 6 cm, 7 cm _____   **c.** 5 cm, 9 cm, 10 cm _____

    d. 7 cm, 3 cm, 4 cm _____   **e.** 2 cm, 10 cm, 4 cm _____   **f.** 4 cm, 8 cm, 4 cm _____

4 Complete the table.

	Length (cm)	Width (cm)	Height (cm)	Volume (cm³)
a.	4	3	2	
b.	2	1	1	
c.	2	2	3	
d.	4	2	1	
e.	4	2	6	
f.	7	3	5	

5 Write three things that are best measured in cubic centimeters.

    a. _____

    b. _____

    c. _____

6 Sketch and label a prism that has a volume of 10 cm³ in the box at the right.

Probability and Arrangements

1 Which of the spinners has the greatest chance of landing on the following colors?

1.   **2.**   **3.**   **4.**   **5.**   **6.**

a. blue (B) _____ **b.** white (W) _____ **c.** red (R) _____

d. orange (O) _____ **e.** green (G) _____ **f.** yellow (Y) _____

2 Are the following correct arrangements of ▲ ▲ ● ■? Write *yes* or *no*.

a. ▲ ● ■ ▲ _____ **b.** ▲ ● ● ■ _____ **c.** ■ ● ▲ ■ _____

d. ■ ● ▲ ▲ _____ **e.** ▲ ● ▲ ■ _____ **f.** ▲ ▲ ■ ● _____

3 Use the scale 0 to 1 to rate the chance of each of the following events happening.

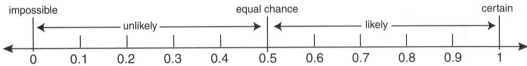

a. I will have a birthday next year. _____

b. I will fly to the moon next week. _____

c. My first toss of a coin will be a head. _____

d. The sun will rise tomorrow. _____

e. My team will win the next soccer game we play. _____

f. Bob's birthday is in a month that starts with *J.* _____

4 Write the probability of each spinner landing on red (R) as a fraction.

a.  _____ **b.**  _____ **c.**  _____ **d.**  _____

5 There are 10 colored balls in the box. State the probability of drawing each color combination as a decimal.

a. red (R)_____ **b.** blue (B) or orange (O)_____

c. yellow (Y)_____ **d.** pink (P) or white (W)_____

e. red (R) or blue (B)_____ **f.** white (W), yellow (Y), or green (G)_____

6 What are all the different possible combinations of rolling 2 standard dice?

_____

_____

_____

Predicting

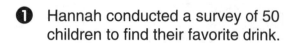

❶ Hannah conducted a survey of 50 children to find their favorite drink.

Milk	Water	Juice	Soda	Smoothie	Other
9	13	8	12	5	3

Use the information to predict how many children out of 100 would prefer the following.

a. water _____

b. soda _____

c. smoothie _____

d. other _____

e. juice _____

f. milk _____

❷ Using the information in question 1, predict how many children out of 1,000 would prefer the following drink.

a. juice _____

b. smoothie _____

c. water _____

d. milk _____

e. soda _____

f. other _____

❸ Fifty children were surveyed to find their favorite color.

red	blue	yellow	green	orange	pink	black
10	9	6	4	4	9	8

Use the information to predict how many children out of 200 would prefer the following.

a. red _____

b. green _____

c. pink _____

d. blue _____

e. yellow _____

f. orange _____

❹ Use the information in question 3 to predict how many children out of 500 would prefer the following color.

a. yellow _____

b. green _____

c. orange _____

d. blue _____

e. black _____

f. pink _____

❺ **a.** Use the information in question 1 to predict how many children out of 100 would prefer milk or water. _____

b. Use the information in question 1 to predict how many children out of 1,000 would prefer soda or smoothie. _____

❻ Draw a tree diagram to show the possibilities of spinning the spinner below three times.

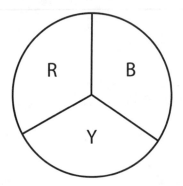

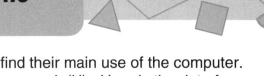

Tables and Graphs

1 Mrs. Jones surveyed all of the students in her class to find their main use of the computer. Their use was email (E), Internet (I), games (G), and homework (H). Here is the data for the class:

E, I, G, I, E, H, I, G, I, E, I, I, H, G, H, E, G, G, E, I, I, H, G, G, E, I, H, H, E, I, G, G, E, G

Computer Use	Tally
email	c.
a.	d.
b.	e.
homework	f.

Create a tally table based on the above information.

2 Using the information in question 1, how many children mainly used the computer for:

a. email? _____   **b.** homework? _____   **c.** games? _____

d. Internet? _____   **e.** email or Internet? _____   **f.** games or homework? _____

3 Use the tally table in question 1 to complete the graph. Be sure to include labels for the graph.

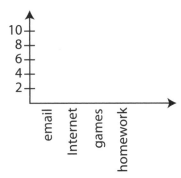

4 Using the graph in question 3, which computer use had:

a. 5 children or more? _____   **b.** 8 children? _____

c. the most children? _____   **d.** the least children? _____

e. less than 8 children? _____   **f.** between 5 and 9 children? _____

5 **a.** What was the total number of children in the class? _____

b. How many children mainly used the computer for activities other than homework? _____

6 **a.** Create a picture graph in the space below to represent the following information, using ▲ = 2 water balloons.

Kids	Water Balloons
Ben	10
Luke	8
Sara	9
Kim	12
Tom	11

b. Make up a question that can be answered by the above graph. Then answer it.

_____

Divided Bar Graphs

1 On the table, there were 30 blocks lined up in a row. Jo drew the divided bar graph below 15 cm long, so each $\frac{1}{2}$ cm stood for one block.

blue	green	yellow	red

Measure in centimeters to determine the length that each color represents on the graph.

a. green blocks _____

b. red blocks _____

c. yellow blocks _____

d. blue blocks _____

e. red or yellow blocks _____

f. blue or green blocks _____

2 What fraction of the graph shows the following?

a. yellow blocks _____

b. red blocks _____

c. blue blocks _____

d. green blocks _____

e. white blocks _____

f. green or yellow blocks _____

3 Of the total number of blocks, how many are:

a. blue? _____

b. red? _____

c. green? _____

d. yellow? _____

e. blue or green? _____

f. green or yellow? _____

4 In a class of 20 students, here are their hair colors:

brown	blonde	black	red
6	8	4	2

Label the divided bar graph for the hair color of the students. Each space represents two students.

5 What fraction of the students have:

a. black or red hair? _____

b. blonde or brown hair? _____

c. brown or black hair? _____

6 In the space below, create a divided bar graph that represents the following.

0.3 = apples	0.4 = bananas	0.2 = pears	0.1 = plums

Pie Charts

1 For a school of 200 students, this is the breakdown of the students' winter sports. Complete the table using the information from the pie chart.

Sport	Fraction	Percent	Number
football	**a.**	37.5%	75
gymnastics	$\frac{1}{8}$	12.5%	**b.**
indoor soccer	**c.**	**d.**	50
basketball	$\frac{1}{4}$	**e.**	**f.**

2 For a school of 200 students, this is the breakdown of the students' summer sports. Complete the table using the information from the pie chart.

	Sport	Fraction	Percent	Number
a.	baseball			
b.	basketball			
c.	tennis			
d.	soccer			
e.	swimming			
f.	softball			

3 Use the information from questions 1 and 2 to answer the following.

   a. How many students play basketball in both winter and summer? _____

   b. Do more students do gymnastics or softball? _____

4 The pie chart represents the cities of origin of 800 people arriving at a Sydney Train Station in Australia. Each section represents 50 people. How many people come from:

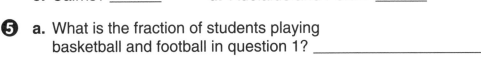

   a. Melbourne? _____   **b.** Brisbane? _____

   c. Cairns? _____   **d.** Adelaide and Perth? _____

5 **a.** What is the fraction of students playing basketball and football in question 1? _____

   b. What is the total number of students playing ball sports in summer and winter in questions 1 and 2? _____

6 Construct a pie chart using the below information. Complete the table to show the number of degrees in the circle that represents each flavor.

	Preferred Ice Cream Flavor	Number	Degrees
a.	chocolate	40	
b.	vanilla	25	
c.	strawberry	20	
d.	caramel	10	
e.	other	5	

Mean, Median, and Graphs

1 Find the mean of each set of measurements.

a. 20 in., 80 in., 60 in., 80 in. _____   **b.** 19 mi., 13 mi., 8 mi., 11 mi., 14 mi. _____

c. 2,428 ft., 3,380 ft., 492 ft. _____   **d.** 38°F, 32°F, 19°F, 25°F, 26°F _____

e. 42 cm, 66 cm, 25 cm, 35 cm, 71 cm, 52 cm _____

f. 650 lb., 880 lb., 475 lb., 495 lb. _____

2 What are the means (correct to one decimal place) of the following scores?

a.

320	640	725	830	955	756

_____

b.

1,128	4,326	4,980	3,620	1,175	2,246

_____

c.

4,280	5,600	6,325	5,920	4,955	6,892

_____

d.

9,980	9,762	9,543	9,029	9,785	9,421	9,360

_____

e.

22,510	23,960	24,785	22,897	27,463	28,486	22,435

_____

f.

41,600	43,900	48,750	50,210	40,740	48,240

_____

3 Complete the table and calculate the mean temperature for the town in the first six days of April.

	Temp. °F	Date
a.		4/1
b.		4/2
c.		4/3
d.		4/4
e.		4/5
f.		4/6

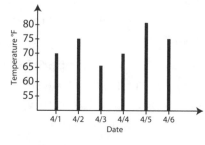

Mean = _____

4 What is the median of the following values?

a. 2, 4, 6, 8, 10 _____   **b.** 1, 3, 5, 7, 9, 11, 13 _____

c. 40, 60, 80, 90, 110 _____   **d.** 1.2, 1.8, 2.3, 3.5, 4.6, 5.2 _____

e. 160, 190, 250, 310, 360 _____   **f.** 320, 450, 490, 510 _____

5 If the temperature on April 7 was 76°F, what is the new mean temperature for the week of the town in question 3?   _____

6 The average of a set of scores is 15. None of the scores is 15 and there are 5 scores. What might these scored be?   _____

1 Water, oil, and detergent were used to fill a 1,000 mL container. In the container, what is the volume of:

a. oil? _____

b. detergent? _____

c. water? _____

What fraction of the container has:

d. water? _____

e. oil? _____

f. detergent? _____

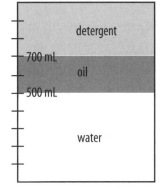

2 Of a survey of 240 people, here is a pie chart of their favorite shapes. What fraction of people chose:

a. triangle? _____   **b.** circle? _____

c. square? _____   **d.** rectangle? _____

e. other? _____

f. square and rectangle? _____

3 Of the results in question 2, how many people chose:

a. circle? _____   **b.** rectangle? _____   **c.** square? _____

d. triangle? _____   **e.** other? _____   **f.** circle and square? _____

4 Of 500 people surveyed, this divided bar graph shows the breakdown of the most popular types of pets. How many people preferred:

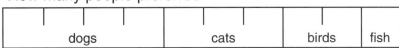

a. cats? _____   **b.** dogs? _____   **c.** birds? _____

d. fish? _____   **e.** dogs and cats? _____   **f.** birds and fish? _____

5 **a.** What fraction of the container in question 1 has oil and detergent? _____

b. What fraction of the people in question 2 chose circles and triangles? _____

c. How many people in question 3 chose rectangles and circles? _____

d. How many people preferred cats, fish, and birds in question 4? _____

6 Draw the container in question 1 as a divided bar graph in the space below.

Line Graphs

❶ Yuko travels 630 miles by car for a work event four times a year. Find the time it takes her to travel:

a. 630 miles. _____

b. 350 miles. _____

c. 140 miles. _____

d. 490 miles. _____

e. 70 miles. _____

f. 280 miles. _____

❷ Find how far Yuko travels in:

a. 1 hour. _____   **b.** 4 hours. _____   **c.** 10 hours. _____

d. 6 hours. _____   **e.** 3 hours. _____   **f.** 7 hours. _____

❸ The table shows the temperature on two days at six different times. Create a line graph, plotting both sets of data on the same graph. Use a different color to represent each day.

Time	Day 1 Temp.	Day 2 Temp.
noon	74°F	77°F
1 p.m.	76°F	78°F
2 p.m.	77°F	79°F
3 p.m.	77°F	82°F
4 p.m.	79°F	83°F
5 p.m.	78°F	83°F

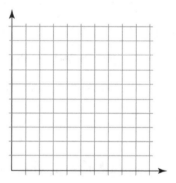

❹ Using the information from question 3, which day had the:

a. greatest temperature at 3 p.m.?_____   **b.** greatest temperature at noon?_____

c. greatest temperature in the afternoon?_____   **d.** lowest temperature in the afternoon? _____

e. greatest increase in temperature in an hour? _____

f. greatest decrease in temperature in an hour? _____

❺ a. How long is Yuko's break after driving 210 miles in question 1?_____

b. What is the largest distance Yuko travels without a break in question 1?_____

c. What is the difference in temperature between day 1 and day 2 at 3 p.m. in question 3?   _____

❻ A walker covers 100 yards every minute and a jogger covers 200 yards every minute. Draw a line graph to show the walker and the jogger's travel over the first 1,000 yards.

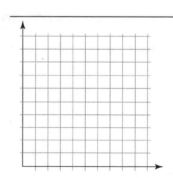

1 Here is a list that represents the number of each type of animal seen at a zoo. Using the list, complete the tally table. The first one has been done for you.

C, K, R, E, M, R, B, K,
M, R, D, C, B, R, K, B,
C, E, R, B, K, M, K, M,
D, B, R, C, K, R, M, B,
R, D, C

	Animal	Tally	Total
	rabbit (R)	||||| |||	8
a.	capybara (C)		
b.	koala (K)		
c.	elephant (E)		
d.	deer (D)		
e.	badger (B)		
f.	monkey (M)		

2 Create a bar graph at the right using the information from question 1.

3 How many of the following animals were there?

a. rabbits and monkeys _____

b. capybaras and deer _____

c. koalas, elephants, and badgers _____

Which type of animal was there:

d. more than 6 of? _____ e. less than 3 of? _____ f. exactly 6 of? _____

4 Use the graph to find the answer to each of the following.

a. $3 \times 6 =$ _____

b. $1.5 \times 6 =$ _____

c. $5 \times 6 =$ _____

d. $2\frac{1}{2} \times 6 =$ _____

e. $3\frac{1}{4} \times 6 =$ _____

f. $2.75 \times 6 =$ _____

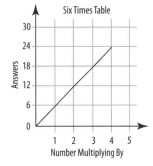

Six Times Table

Answers

Number Multiplying By

5 a. What is the total number of animals counted in question 1? _____

b. What is 3.5×6 using the graph in question 4? _____

6 Draw a line graph for the first five of the 9 times table.

Reading Graphs

1 The eye color of Mr. Williams' students was noted and the following graph produced. How many of his students have:

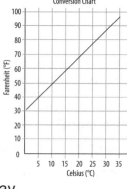

a. brown eyes?_____ **b.** hazel eyes?_____

c. green eyes?_____

Which category had: **d.** the least number of students?_____

e. the most number of students?_____ **f.** between 6 and 12 students?_____

2 The following graph allows us to convert between Celsius and Fahrenheit temperatures. Use the graph to convert:

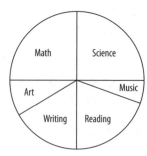

a. 10°C to °F. _____

b. 35°C to °F. _____

c. 90°F to °C. _____

Circle the greater temperature?

d. 5°C or 35°F   **e.** 20°C or 70°F   **f.** 80°F or 25°C

3 Jordan drew a pie graph to show what she did during her school day.

a. What activities took up the most time?_____

b. What activity took up the least time?_____

c. Was more time spent reading or doing art?_____

d. Which activity was closest in length to reading?_____

e. Was less time spent in reading or math?_____

f. Which sections each used $\frac{1}{4}$ of the school day?_____

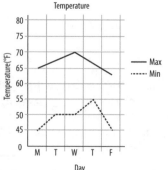

4 What was the:

a. maximum temperature for Friday?_____

b. maximum temperature for Wednesday?_____

c. minimum temperature for Monday?_____

d. minimum temperature for Wednesday?_____

e. day that had the least difference between maximum and minimum temperature?_____

5 **a.** What was the total number of students surveyed in question 1?_____

b. Which two activities in question 3 use the least amount of time?_____

6 List one advantage and one disadvantage of a pie chart.

_____

_____

Collected Data

1 Use the population graph to answer the following.

Population

When did the population reach:

a. 5 million?_____

b. 10 million?_____

c. 15 million? _____

When was the population approximately:

d. 7 million? _____ **e.** 12 million? _____ **f.** 18 million? _____

2 Approximately, what was the population:

a. in 1930? _____

b. in 1980? _____

c. in 1990? _____

d. in 2000? _____

e. difference between 1900 and 2000?_____ **f.** difference between 1900 and 1950?____

3 Here is a table of the totals of different insect types. Complete the tally table.

	Insect Type	Tally	Total
a.	butterfly		9
b.	ant		14
c.	fly		8
d.	flea		13
e.	grasshopper		5
f.	beetle		12

4 Construct a bar graph using the information from question 3.

5 **a.** Using the graph in question 1, what ten-year period had the greatest population growth? _____

b. What was the total number of insects found in question 3? _____

c. Which type of insect had more than 13 found in question 4? _____

6 Use 2 coins and collect 20 pieces of information. Create a tally chart and graph your results.

Problem Solving — Inverse Operations

1 Find the missing numbers.

a. 46 + 19 = 50 + ☐

b. 198 + 245 = 360 + ☐

c. 56 + 135 = 126 + ☐

d. 328 + ☐ = 109 + 248

e. 411 + ☐ = 512 + 346

f. 245 + ☐ = 456 + 173

2 Find the missing numbers.

a. 4 × 70 = 560 ÷ ☐

b. 90 ÷ ☐ = 5 × 6

c. 1,210 ÷ ☐ = 10 × 11

d. 49 ÷ ☐ = 350 ÷ 50

e. 12 × ☐ = 432 ÷ 3

f. 75 ÷ 3 = 5 × ☐

3 Find the missing numbers.

a. 3 + ☐ = 8 − 5

b. 7 × ☐ = 14 × 2

c. 100 ÷ ☐ = 25 − 5

d. 144 ÷ 6 = 6 × ☐

e. 45 + 11 = 7 × ☐

f. 198 − ☐ = 12 × 11

4 What was the starting number if I:

a. subtracted 6, multiplied by 5, then added 9 to get 34? _____

b. multiplied by 8, added 429, divided by 5 to get 105?_____

c. added 57, multiplied by 2, divided by 20 to get 11?_____

d. divided by 3, added 17, multiplied by 3 to get 90?_____

e. subtracted 248, divided by 4, subtracted 100 to get 88? _____

f. multiplied by 7, added 20, divided by 30 to get 10?_____

5 Forty-six plus what number is equal to nine multiplied by six? Write this number in words.

_____

6 Fifteen boxes were placed in rows to form a triangle. One box was at the top row. How many boxes were in the bottom row?

_____

Problem Solving — Money

1 I recently bought some plants for my vegetable garden. I bought 6 strawberry plants for $4.86, a tomato plant for $2.35, a packet of 20 carrot seeds for $6.50, a box of 8 lettuce plants for $7.52, and a small lemon tree for $10.15.

   a. How much was each strawberry plant? _____

   b. How much was each lettuce plant? _____

   c. Which single plant cost the most? _____

   d. What was the total cost of the lemon tree and tomato plant? _____

   e. If only 13 carrots grew, how much did each one cost? _____

2 Doreen gets paid $11.25 an hour. If she works for 5 hours, circle the correct pay.

   a. $54.95   **b.** $53.50   **c.** $55.75

   d. $55.00   **e.** $52.15   **f.** $56.25

3 Calculate the following.

   a. $3 \times \$7.56 =$ _____   **b.** $\$46.20 \div 2 =$ _____

   c. $\$15.75 + \$4.85 =$ _____   **d.** $\$40.00 - \$16.85 =$ _____

   e. $\$100 - \$78.22 =$ _____   **f.** $\$20.15 + \$2.75 + \$3.20 =$ _____

4 Find the missing amount.

   a. $3.26 + $4.30 + ☐ = $10.00   **b.** $75.26 + $11.15 + ☐ = $100.00

   c. $50.25 = $42.98 + $1.56 + ☐   **d.** $32.48 = $11.37 + $12.65 + ☐

   e. $75.50 = $100.00 − ☐   **f.** $45.52 = $70.85 − ☐

5 What was the total cost of all of the items in question 1? _____

6 Write a word problem that has the answer $11.17.

_____

_____

Problem Solving — Critical Thinking

1 Hats are placed in a straight line one yard apart. Find how many hats are used if the line extends:

a. 10 yards _____

b. 85 yards _____

c. 36 yards _____

d. 47 yards _____

e. What is the pattern? _____

2 I have 8 colored pencils that vary in length from 14.7 cm to 17.3 cm. Circle the amount which could be the total of their lengths.

a. 96.7 cm

b. 112.9 cm

c. 111.9 cm

d. 125.5 cm

e. 116.7 cm

f. 140.2 cm

3 Object A has a weight of 160 lb., Object B has a weight of 250 lb., and Object C has a weight of 190 lb. Object D has a weight more than A but less than C. Which of the following could be the total weight of the four objects?

a. 550 lb.

b. 690 lb.

c. 710 lb.

d. 740 lb.

e. 770 lb.

f. 790 lb.

4 Object A has a weight of 120 lb. and Object B has a weight of 190 lb. Object C has a weight more than A but less than B. Which of the following could be the total weight of the three objects?

a. 420 lb.

b. 475 lb.

c. 510 lb.

5 Children link hands to form a chain. Find how many total hands are held if there are:

a. 3 children in the chain. _____

b. 6 children in the chain. _____

c. 10 children in the chain. _____

d. 15 children in the chain. _____

6 A snail is climbing a wall that is 21 yards high. It climbs up 4 yards every day and slides down 3 yards every night. How many days does it take the snail to reach the top of the wall? _____

Addition and Subtraction Practice

❶ Add the following.

a. 42,146 + 38,491 + 2,468 _____

b. 1,076 + 49,830 + 211,063 _____

c. 110,439 + 204,117 + 841,735 _____

d. 1,096,423 + 408,291 + 441,055 _____

e. 4,639,805 + 221,176 + 449,851 _____

f. 369,725 + 11,063 + 1,185 _____

❷ Subtract the following.

a.
```
  9,000
- 4,287
```

b.
```
  10,000
-  1,569
```

c.
```
  30,000
- 26,483
```

d.
```
  22,000
- 14,892
```

e.
```
  140,000
-  26,487
```

f.
```
  321,000
-  46,987
```

❸ Add the following.

a.
```
  846,931
  257,486
+ 110,798
```

b.
```
  421,103
   96,467
   11,042
+   4,385
```

c.
```
  463,981
   24,836
   44,997
+  10,436
```

d.
```
  468,925
  110,763
   43,685
+  11,994
```

❹ Complete the missing numbers.

a.
```
  96,2_6
- 3_,52_
  _7,_25
```

b.
```
  _2,_80
- 19,8_3
  2_,81_
```

c.
```
  _3,_79
-  _,84_
  6,7_0
```

d.
```
  21,_9_
- 1_,3_6
   3,136
```

❺ In one large container, there were 1,437 oranges. In another container, there were 1,989 oranges. 2,500 of the oranges were sold to grocery stores. How many oranges were left in the containers? _____

❻ In one week, James deposited into his account $348 and $526. He also withdrew $249, $399, and $107. At the end of the week, did James' account increase or decrease and by how much? _____

Multiplication and Division Practice

1 Multiply the following.

  a.   4 3 8
       ×   2 0

  b.   6 9 1
       ×   4 0

  c.   4 2 6
       ×   6 0

  d.   3 , 2 4 8
       ×   3 0

  e.   1 , 4 6 9
       ×   5 0

  f.   2 , 4 8 7
       ×   8 0

2 Divide the following.

  a. $60\overline{)4,285}$

  b. $70\overline{)1,107}$

  c. $50\overline{)3,560}$

  d. $80\overline{)2,448}$

  e. $20\overline{)4,165}$

  f. $30\overline{)1,109}$

3 Multiply the following.

  a. 29 × 47 = _____

  b. 46 × 33 = _____

  c. 62 × 81 = _____

  d. 19 × 36 = _____

  e. 24 × 44 = _____

  f. 95 × 86 = _____

4 Divide the following. Write answers with remainders in fraction form.

  a. $4\overline{)37,980}$

  b. $9\overline{)911,763}$

  c. $8\overline{)42,116}$

  d. $7\overline{)43,684}$

  e. $5\overline{)21,104}$

  f. $3\overline{)278,496}$

5 A group of 144 items is called a *gross*. How many items would be in 73 gross? _____

6 479 packages of 6 cookies in each package need to be divided evenly into 3 crates. If you take the cookies out of each package, how many cookies can you put in each crate? _____

Fractions Practice

1 Complete the equivalent fractions.

   a. $\frac{5}{9} = \frac{\square}{18}$
      b. $\frac{6}{10} = \frac{18}{\square}$
      c. $\frac{2}{3} = \frac{\square}{30}$

   d. $\frac{80}{100} = \frac{\square}{10}$
     e. $\frac{49}{56} = \frac{7}{\square}$
      f. $\frac{35}{50} = \frac{\square}{10}$

2 Find the following.

   a. $\frac{2}{5}$ of 20 _____
      b. $\frac{3}{4}$ of 48 _____

   c. $\frac{5}{9}$ of 45 _____
      d. $\frac{2}{7}$ of 84 _____

   e. $\frac{2}{3}$ of 27 _____
      f. $\frac{5}{6}$ of 60 _____

3 Add or subtract the fractions. Simplify the answers.

   a. $\frac{2}{5} + \frac{7}{10} =$ _____
      b. $\frac{6}{9} - \frac{1}{3} =$ _____

   c. $\frac{5}{10} + \frac{2}{3} =$ _____
      d. $2 - \frac{5}{6} =$ _____

   e. $\frac{3}{4} + \frac{5}{16} =$ _____
      f. $\frac{9}{12} - \frac{1}{4} =$ _____

4 Multiply the fractions.

   a. $\frac{3}{5} \times \frac{2}{3} =$ _____
      b. $\frac{4}{10} \times \frac{2}{3} =$ _____

   c. $\frac{5}{6} \times \frac{1}{7} =$ _____
      d. $\frac{3}{4} \times \frac{5}{8} =$ _____

   e. $\frac{1}{4} \times \frac{8}{9} =$ _____
      f. $\frac{2}{7} \times \frac{1}{2} =$ _____

5 Complete the table.

	Question	Repeated Addition	Fraction	Mixed Number
a.	$3 \times \frac{2}{5}$			
b.	$3 \times \frac{5}{8}$			
c.	$2 \times \frac{2}{3}$			
d.	$2 \times \frac{7}{10}$			
e.	$8 \times \frac{1}{6}$			
f.	$10 \times \frac{3}{4}$			

6 Draw a diagram to show 4 groups of $\frac{3}{4}$ and find the answer.

Decimals Practice

1 Add the decimals.

a. 4.601
   +2.4

b. 9.365
   +2.194

c. 11.245
   + 9.67

d. 18.246
   +13.487

e. 21.486
   +19.577

f. 36.98
   +21.073

2 Find the difference between the following.

a. 5 and 2.18 _____

b. 9 and 7.365 _____

c. 4 and 3.467 _____

d. 21 and 14.921 _____

e. 14 and 9.625 _____

f. 11 and 10.739 _____

3 Multiply the following.

a. $4.21
   x   3

b. $9.75
   x   6

c. $8.32
   x   4

d. $9.98
   x   2

e. $2.75
   x   8

f. $1.99
   x   7

4 Divide the following.

a. 4.62 ÷ 10 = _____

b. 9.265 ÷ 100 = _____

c. 21.48 ÷ 1,000 = _____

d. 123.245 ÷ 1,000 = _____

e. 49.3 ÷ 10 = _____

f. 0.46 ÷ 100 = _____

5 Becky's mom timed Becky to see how fast she could change her clothes. In the morning, it took Becky 9.2 seconds to change into her school clothes. At night, it took her 7.3 seconds to change into her pajamas. What was Becky's average time? _____

6 Jorge has four hundred thirty-five dimes and ninety-two silver dollars. How much money does Jorge have? _____

Answer Key

Page 7
1. **a.** 521,702   **b.** 900,576   **c.** 250,820
   d. 611,465   **e.** 108,239   **f.** 95,891

2.

	HTh	TTh	Th	H	T	O
a.	5	2	1	7	0	2
b.	9	0	0	5	7	6
c.	2	5	0	8	2	0
d.	6	1	1	4	6	5
e.	1	0	8	2	3	9
f.		9	5	8	9	1

3. **a.** 80   **b.** 6   **c.** 700,000
   d. 8,000   **e.** 70,000   **f.** 600
4. **a.** 742,115; 742,215; 742,315
   b. 907,126; 907,136; 907,146
   c. 852,105; 862,105; 872,105
   d. 223,467; 323,467; 423,467
5. **a.** one hundred ten thousand, seven hundred ninety-three
   b. two hundred forty-eight thousand, nine hundred sixteen
6. 1,000,000; 998,000; 996,000; 994,000; 992,000; 990,000; 988,000; 986,000

Page 8
1. **a.**

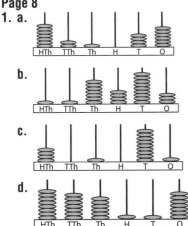

   b.

   c.

   d.

2. **a.** eighty thousand, four hundred eleven
   b. nine hundred ninety-eight thousand, six hundred forty-two
   c. eight hundred seventy thousand, four hundred
3. **a.** <   **b.** >   **c.** >
   d. <   **e.** <   **f.** <
4. **a.** 19,221   **b.** 198,921   **c.** 51,010
   d. 89,270   **e.** 24,879   **f.** 456,285
5. **a.** 4   **b.** 23   **c.** 204   **d.** 219
6. 7,896

Page 9
1. **a.** 5   **b.** 5,000,000   **c.** 5,000
   d. 500,000   **e.** 5,000   **f.** 50,000
2. **a.** 1,243,819; 1,308,925; 1,346,721
   b. 2,487,905; 2,635,921; 2,711,809
   c. 4,105,907; 4,246,385; 4,365,111
3. **a.** 8,051,987; 7,921,300; 7,621,505
   b. 5,296,837; 5,121,352; 5,021,486
   c. 8,110,425; 7,932,481; 6,842,859
4. **a.** 2,000,000   **b.** 6,000,000   **c.** 1,000,000
   d. 1,000,000   **e.** 8,000,000   **f.** 5,000,000

5. **a.** ten thousands place; 90,000
   b. millions place; 8,000,000
   c. hundreds place; 700
   d. thousands place; 7,000
   e. millions place; 1,000,000
   f. ten millions place; 20,000,000
6. **a.** 50,000,000   **b.** 50,000,000   **c.** 60,000,000

Page 10
1. **a.** 63, 72   **b.** 75, 85   **c.** 45, 55
   d. 68, 78   **e.** 10, 8, 7   **f.** 1, $1\frac{1}{2}$, 2
2. **a.** 1st number × 9   **b.** 1st number + 19
   c. 1st number × 10   **d.** 1st number − 8
   e. 1st number ÷ 7   **f.** 1st number ÷ 2
3. **a.** 12, 17, 23   **b.** 7, 9.5, 12.5
   c. 37, 26, 17   **d.** 32, 47, 65
4. **a.** +1, +2, +3, +4, +5, +6
   b. +0.5, +1, +1.5, +2, +2.5, +3
   c. −19, −17, −15, −13, −11, −9
   d. +3, +6, +9, +12, +15, +18
5. **a.** 1, 4, 9, 16 (1^2, 2^2, 3^2, 4^2)   **b.** $10^2 = 100$
6. 9, 13, 17, 21, 25, 29, 33

Page 11
1. **a.** 142,561   **b.** 608,096   **c.** 453,785   **d.** 870,807
2. **a.** 50,000 + 6,000 + 400 + 9
   b. 200,000 + 10,000 + 3,000 + 800 + 40 + 7
   c. 400,000 + 60,000 + 2,000 + 1
   d. 1,000,000 + 900,000 + 5,000 + 600 + 20 + 1
3. **a.** 428   **b.** 917   **c.** 4,863
   d. 2,748   **e.** 21,368   **f.** 72,499
4. **a.** 4   **b.** 21   **c.** 92
   d. 847   **e.** 123   **f.** 1,428
5. **a.** <   **b.** <
6. **a.** true   **b.** false

Page 12
1. **a.** XLVII   **b.** LXXXVI   **c.** XCIX
   d. CCCLXVIII   **e.** MCCL   **f.** MMMDCCXLI
2. **a.** 34   **b.** 43   **c.** 260
   d. 2,100   **e.** 462   **f.** 1,910
3. **a.** III, VI, IX, XII   **b.** XXIX   **c.** LXXVIII
   d. MMII   **e.** XIV   **f.** MCMXC
4. **a.** XL, L   **b.** LXV, LXX   **c.** CD, D   **d.** MMD, MMM
5. Answers will vary.
6. Check clocks for accuracy. Times will vary.

Page 13
1. **a.** 110   **b.** 120   **c.** 120
   d. 1,000   **e.** 900   **f.** 1,500
2. **a.** 195   **b.** 394   **c.** 913
   d. 285   **e.** 193   **f.** 351
3. **a.** 400 + 400 = 800   **b.** 500 + 300 = 800
   c. 900 + 300 = 1,200   **d.** 1,000 + 300 = 1,300
   e. 1,400 + 500 = 1,900   **f.** 2,400 + 900 = 3,300
4. **a.** 1,412   **b.** 1,423   **c.** 9,083
   d. 13,655   **e.** 7,764   **f.** 8,267
5. 67,314 people
6. Word problems will vary. 2,147 + 8,736 = 10,883

Page 14
1. **a.** 1,760   **b.** 1,443   **c.** 2,215
   d. 4,935   **e.** 13,538   **f.** 17,134
2. **a.** $58,661   **b.** $129,977   **c.** $861,081
   d. $178,602   **e.** $785,333   **f.** $1,018,256
3. **a.**
$$35,5\underline{6}4 + 4,8\underline{4}5 = 4\underline{0},409$$
b.
$$632,9\underline{8}6 + 201,264 = 83\underline{4},250$$
c.
$$107,9\underline{3}2 + 4\underline{6}5,187 = 57\underline{3},119$$
   d.
$$46\underline{7},326 + 42\underline{2},736 = \underline{8}90,062$$
e.
$$32\underline{9},184 + 462,773 = 79\underline{1},957$$
f.
$$6\underline{2}7,854 + 256,43\underline{7} = 884,2\underline{9}1$$
4. **a.** $10,050   **b.** 85,763 boxes   **c.** 1,476 sheets
5. 1,003,961
6. $118,520

Page 15
1. **a.** 1,511,935   **b.** 1,478,643   **c.** 1,122,143
   d. 1,649,274   **e.** 1,339,666   **f.** 938,838
2. **a.** 6,235,754   **b.** 2,276,103
   c. 11,528,000   **d.** 13,730,000
3. **a.** $644,688.43   **b.** $5,653,635.79
   c. $11,284,181.38   **d.** $2,400,878.60
4. **a.** 21,702 inches   **b.** 85,294 pounds
   c. 1,549,522 feet
5. $35,085
6. 1,031,919.1; one million, thirty-one thousand, nine hundred nineteen and one tenth

Page 16
1. **a.** 427   **b.** 834   **c.** 374   **d.** 261   **e.** 139   **f.** 519
2. **a.** 4,622   **b.** 884   **c.** 271   **d.** 2,887   **e.** 1,638   **f.** 606
3. **a.**
$$5,617 - 4,313 = 1,3\underline{0}4$$
b.
$$5,1\underline{6}4 - 3,127 = 2,037$$
c.
$$9,541 - 2,672 = 6,86\underline{9}$$
   d.
$$8,76\underline{3} - 2,40\underline{8} = 6,3\underline{5}5$$
e.
$$8,\underline{5}70 - 723 = 7,847$$
f.
$$8,200 - 7,004 = 1,196$$
4. **a.** 2,401   **b.** 7,252   **c.** 5,520   **d.** 5,484   **e.** 842   **f.** 2,281
5. $807 profit
6. 547 stamps

Page 17
1. **a.** 50   **b.** 60   **c.** 100   **d.** 110   **e.** 260   **f.** 490
2. **a.** 100   **b.** 400   **c.** 900   **d.** 1,300   **e.** 5,000   **f.** 4,500
3. **a.** 1,000   **b.** 1,000   **c.** 3,000
   d. 18,000   **e.** 30,000   **f.** 126,000
4. **a.** 6,000 + 4,000; 10,000   **b.** 3,000 + 3,000; 6,000
   c. 1,000 + 3,000; 4,000   **d.** 36,000 + 6,000; 42,000
   e. 55,000 + 5,000; 60,000   **f.** 10,000 + 27,000; 37,000
5. **a.** 9K   **b.** 14K   **c.** 21K   **d.** 51K   **e.** 37K   **f.** 85K
6. **a.** true   **b.** false   **c.** false   **d.** true

Page 18
1. **a.** 36,461   **b.** 44,237   **c.** 37,719
   d. 34,640   **e.** 25,270   **f.** 4,250
2. **a.** 47,000 − 21,000 = 26,000
   b. 83,000 − 68,000 = 15,000
   c. 92,000 − 43,000 = 49,000
   d. 67,000 − 41,000 = 26,000
   e. 60,000 − 17,000 = 43,000
   f. 43,000 − 11,000 = 32,000

3. **a.** 554,406 inches   **b.** 366,568 feet
   c. 123,433 miles
4. **a.** 780,838   **b.** 341,597   **c.** 26,966
   d. 252,781   **e.** 488,463   **f.** 222,055
5. $62,713
6. Word problems will vary.

Page 19
1. **a.** 1,254,000   **b.** 6,686,000   **c.** 3,528,000
   d. 1,889,000   **e.** 4,529,000   **f.** 1,049,000
2. **a.** $3,923,225   **b.** $2,926,290   **c.** $517,253
   d. $4,462,314   **e.** $1,970,304   **f.** $1,822,528
3. **a.** 97,940 mi.^{2} **b.** 99,629 mi.^{2} **c.** 257,649 mi.^{2}
   d. 95,891 mi.^{2} **e.** 394,687 mi.^{2} **f.** 12,180 mi.^{2}
4. **a.** 310,713 feet   **b.** $582,756
   c. 705,313 pounds
5. 660,778 mi.^{2} (AK − DE)
6. Answers will vary.

Page 20
1. **a.** 46,200 + 38,000 = 84,200
   b. 17,600 + 19,300 = 36,900
   c. 24,800 + 46,000 = 70,800
   d. 142,900 + 173,100 = 316,000
   e. 429,100 + 140,300 = 569,400
   f. 873,100 + 117,800 = 990,900
2. **a.** 42,000 − 20,000 = 22,000
   b. 26,000 − 8,000 = 18,000
   c. 47,000 − 34,000 = 13,000
   d. 129,000 − 114,000 = 15,000
   e. 168,000 − 123,000 = 45,000
   f. 850,000 − 328,000 = 522,000
3. **a.** $422 + $62 = $484   **b.** $122 + $157 = $279
   c. $643 + $249 = $892   **d.** $479 − $136 = $343
   e. $846 − $138 = $708   **f.** $649 − $378 = $271
4. **a.** 4,300 + 2,000 = 6,300   **b.** 7,400 + 1,300 = 8,700
   c. 8,800 + 4,100 = 12,900   **d.** 4,900 + 4,000 = 8,900
   e. 6,200 + 7,500 = 13,700   **f.** 9,600 + 1,000 = 10,600
5. 2,144,000 − 1,794,000 = 350,000
6. 721,000 + 385,000 = 1,106,000

Page 21
1. **a.** 24   **b.** 60   **c.** 72   **d.** 21   **e.** 60   **f.** 0
2. **a.** 28   **b.** 120   **c.** 40   **d.** 100   **e.** 42   **f.** 36
3. **a.** 3   **b.** 9   **c.** 8   **d.** 7   **e.** 4   **f.** 12
4. **a.** $90   **b.** $12   **c.** $84   **d.** $15   **e.** $24   **f.** $32
5. **a.** true   **b.** false   **c.** false
   d. true   **e.** false   **f.** true
6.

A wheel diagram labeled × 11 with outer values: 88, 0, 99, 110, 132, 77, 66, 121 and inner ring values: 8, 0, 9, 10, 12, 7, 6, 11.

Answer Key

Page 22
1. **a.** 63 **b.** 16 **c.** 55 **d.** 144
2. **a.** 96 **b.** 0 **c.** 28 **d.** 45 **e.** 35 **f.** 6
3. **a.** 2; 12 **b.** 8; 12 **c.** 8; 24 **d.** 30; 10 **e.** 18; 3 **f.** 4; 20
4. **a.** twenty-seven **b.** forty-eight
   c. seven **d.** one hundred thirty-two
   e. one hundred eight **f.** zero
5. **a.** 42 days **b.** 14 days **c.** 70 days
   d. 21 days **e.** 56 days **f.** 49 days
6. 60 cows + 6 horses + 4 pigs + 50 chickens = 120 animals

Page 23
1. **a.** 8 **b.** 27 **c.** 42 **d.** 25 **e.** 32 **f.** 56
2. **a.** 280 **b.** 480 **c.** 5,400
   d. 3,500 **e.** 32,000 **f.** 30,000
3. **a.** 230; 460; 690
   b. 140; 280; 420
   c. 760; 1,520; 2,280
   d. 700; 1,400; 2,100
   e. 400; 800; 1,200
   f. 800; 1,600; 2,400
4. **a.** 400; 4,000; 40,000
   b. 700; 7,000; 70,000
   c. 830; 8,300; 83,000
   d. 290; 2,900; 29,000
   e. 2,000; 20,000; 200,000
   f. 1,670; 16,700; 167,000
5. **a.** 1,200 books **b.** 600 students
   c. 3,600 words **d.** 42,300 pencils
   e. 126,000 stars **f.** 47,000 balls
6. 20 × 89 = 1,780 snacks − (20 × 15 = 300 sold) = 1,480 left

Page 24
1. **a.** 84 **b.** 57 **c.** 378 **d.** 185 **e.** 441 **f.** 324
2. **a.** 447 **b.** 1,032 **c.** 1,505 **d.** 4,950 **e.** 4,998 **f.** 4,416
3. **a.** 8,622 **b.** 7,443 **c.** 32,204
   d. 5,960 **e.** 32,112 **f.** 7,364
4. **a.** 14,580 **b.** 36,960 **c.** 5,350
   d. 121,800 **e.** 387,000 **f.** 36,000
5. **a.** 3,600 seconds
   b. 21,600 seconds
   c. 36,000 seconds
6. 686 stickers

Page 25
1. **a.** 260 × 4 = 1,040 **b.** 830 × 6 = 4,980
   c. 710 × 7 = 4,970 **d.** 550 × 8 = 4,400
2. **a.** 793 **b.** 1,081 **c.** 1,682
   d. 30; 2; 2,432 **e.** 10; 7; 1,071 **f.** 40; 3; 3,655
3. **a.** 1,260 + 441 = 1,701
   b. 4,350 + 261 = 4,611
   c. 2,880 + 672 = 3,552
   d. 1,040 + 182 = 1,222
   e. 1,560 + 156 = 1,716
   f. 2,120 + 265 = 2,385
4. **a.** 12,750 **b.** 34,320 **c.** 41,750
   d. 23,133 **e.** 6,734 **f.** 5,029
5. $8,085
6. 1,126 × 37 = 41,662

Page 26
1. **a.** 120; 1,200; 12,000 **b.** 630; 6,300; 63,000
   c. 1,200; 12,000; 120,000
2. **a.**
$$\begin{array}{r} 2\,1\,5 \\ +\ \ 8\,6\,0 \\ \hline 1\,,0\,7\,5 \end{array}$$
   b.
$$\begin{array}{r} 5\,8\,4 \\ +2\,,9\,2\,0 \\ \hline 3\,,5\,0\,4 \end{array}$$

   c.
$$\begin{array}{rl} 1\,4\,0 & (5 \times 2\,8) \\ +1\,,9\,6\,0 & (70 \times 2\,8) \\ \hline 2\,,1\,0\,0 \end{array}$$

   d.
$$\begin{array}{rl} 1\,1\,1 & (3 \times 3\,7) \\ +1\,,8\,5\,0 & (50 \times 3\,7) \\ \hline 1\,,9\,6\,1 \end{array}$$

3. **a.** 28,882 **b.** 66,872 **c.** 7,696 **d.** 46,782
4. **a.** $1,666 **b.** $4,984 **c.** $5,280
   d. $3,276 **e.** $2,720 **f.** $3,220
5. **a.** 32 **b.** 65 **c.** 26 **d.** 27
6. ($32 + $5) x 12 months = $444 per year

Page 27
1. **a.** 302; 682; 6,234
   b. 735; 828; 1,143; 7,827; 23,412
   c. 536; 984; 1,364; 26,424
   d. 105; 1,700; 9,515
   e. 256; 984; 6,456
   f. 198; 1,368; 9,981; 12,420
2. **a.** true **b.** false **c.** false **d.** true **e.** false **f.** true
3. **a.** 1, 12, 2, 6, 3, 4 **b.** 1, 18, 2, 9, 3, 6
   c. 1, 24, 2, 12, 3, 8, 4, 6 **d.** 1, 30, 2, 15, 3, 10, 5, 6
   e. 1, 48, 2, 24, 3, 16, 4, 12, 6, 8
   f. 1, 60, 2, 30, 3, 20, 4, 15, 5, 12, 6, 10
4. **a.** 7, 14, 21, 28, 35, 42, 49, 56
   b. 6, 12, 18, 24, 30, 36, 42, 48
   c. 11, 22, 33, 44, 55, 66, 77, 88
   d. 12, 24, 36, 48, 60, 72, 84, 96
   e. 10, 20, 30, 40, 50, 60, 70, 80
   f. 8, 16, 24, 32, 40, 48, 56, 64
5. Numbers that end in 0 are divisible by 10.
6. 1, 1,000, 2, 500, 4, 250, 5, 200, 8, 125, 10, 100, 20, 50, 25, 40

Page 28
1. **a.** 30 × 6 = 180 **b.** 50 × 7 = 350 **c.** 50 × 5 = 250
   d. 100 × 9 = 900 **e.** 200 × 8 = 1,600 **f.** 300 × 4 = 1,200
2. **a.** 80 × 20 = 1,600 **b.** 50 × 30 = 1,500
   c. 40 × 60 = 2,400 **d.** 40 × 20 = 800
   e. 50 × 70 = 3,500 **f.** 30 × 70 = 2,100
3. **a.** 80 × 400 = 32,000 **b.** 80 × 700 = 56,000
   c. 20 × 500 = 10,000 **d.** 10 × 600 = 6,000
   e. 40 × 600 = 24,000 **f.** 60 × 900 = 54,000
4. Estimates may vary.
   a. E = 30,000 A = 29,281
   b. E = 16,000 A = 14,688
   c. E = 9,000 A = 11,303
   d. E = 14,000 A = 14,076
   e. E = 12,000 A = 13,317
   f. E = 15,000 A = 11,475
5. 23 x 379 ≈ 20 x 400 = 8,000 newspapers
6. 17 x 14 ≈ 20 x 10 = 200 pages

Answer Key

Page 29
1. a. 9, 8   b. 6, 5   c. 7, 4   d. 12, 8   e. 8, 6   f. 12, 3
2. a. 9   b. 8   c. 1   d. 8   e. 7   f. 10
3. a. 2   b. 9   c. 10   d. 12   e. 8   f. 9
4. a. 32   b. 9   c. 12   d. 23   e. 22   f. 12
5. 41 pencils
6. 5 donut holes

Page 30
1. a. 6   b. 4   c. 3   d. 12   e. 2   f. 8
2. a. 4 r4   b. 3 r3   c. 2 r6   d. 2 r4   e. 1 r4   f. 2 r2
3. a. 60   b. 90   c. 40   d. 50   e. 50   f. 40
4. a. 7, 2   b. 7, 2   c. 9, 2   d. 4, 4   e. 5, 5   f. 10, 3
5. a. 32   b. 14   c. 28   d. 60
6. Word problems will vary.

Page 31
1. a. 8 r4   b. 13 r1   c. 7 r7   d. 4 r6   e. 6 r8   f. 8 r2
2. a. 324   b. 123   c. 112   d. 122   e. 132   f. 126
3. a. 72 r2   b. 65 r5   c. 109 r2
   d. 330 r4   e. 3,008 r2   f. 303 r8
4. a. $46.50
   b. 82 cartons (5 eggs left over)
   c. 159 cars (3 tires left over)
   d. 1,342 thumbtacks (1 left over)
5. (48 + 38 + 52 + 64) ÷ 4 = 50.5 cm
6. 8 cupcakes (5 x 12 = 60 total cupcakes − 4 left = 56 sold ÷ 7 customers = 8 cupcakes for each customer)

Page 32
1. a. 1   b. 1   c. 2   d. 1   e. 2   f. 4
2. a. $21 \frac{1}{2}$ b. $10 \frac{1}{3}$ c. $7 \frac{1}{4}$
   d. $13 \frac{2}{6} = 13 \frac{1}{3}$ e. $18 \frac{4}{5}$ f. $7 \frac{1}{7}$
3. a. $150 \frac{2}{6} = 150 \frac{1}{3}$ b. $125 \frac{3}{4}$ c. $89 \frac{6}{7}$
   d. $74 \frac{2}{8} = 74 \frac{1}{4}$ e. $28 \frac{4}{9}$ f. $86 \frac{3}{5}$
4. a. $1,210 \frac{5}{6}$ b. $1,206 \frac{2}{8} = 1,206 \frac{1}{4}$
   c. $1,823 \frac{2}{3}$ d. $1,335 \frac{5}{7}$
   e. $274 \frac{2}{9}$ f. $1,340 \frac{3}{4}$
5. a. $\frac{7}{10}$ b. $\frac{1}{4}$ c. $\frac{5}{7}$
6. $247 ÷ 3 = 82 \frac{1}{3}$

Page 33
1. a. 39   b. 85   c. 40   d. 67 r1   e. 34 r9   f. 85
2. a. 1,045   b. 1,011   c. 912   d. 1,202   e. 703   f. 2,090
3. a. $503 \frac{1}{4}$ b. $1,403 \frac{4}{5}$ c. 535
   d. $10,200 \frac{1}{3}$ e. $8,826 \frac{7}{8}$ f. 6,017
4. a. 709 in each row   b. $195 each
   c. 207 in each pile   d. 507 box trays
5. 51,523
6. 1,201 weeks

Page 34
1. a. 430.1   b. 743.8   c. 506   d. 849.7   e. 663.5   f. 901
2. a. 436   b. 2,107   c. 4,600   d. 2,104   e. 3,911   f. 6,127
3. a. 2,468   b. 7,102   c. 8,763
   d. 19,041.6   e. 48,795.1   f. 84,731.5
4. a. 960 cm   b. 1,750 cm   c. 49 cm
   d. 871 cm   e. 3,842 cm   f. 112 cm
5. 471
6. 35,000 boxes

Page 35
1. a. 576   b. 249   c. 310   d. 2,300   e. 4,690   f. 4,870
2. a. 21   b. 37   c. 29   d. 480   e. 520   f. 390
3. a. 21 (105 ÷ 5)   b. 120 (360 ÷ 3)   c. 70 (280 ÷ 4)
   d. 600 (4,200 ÷ 7)   e. 119 (1,071 ÷ 9)   f. 30 (180 ÷ 6)
4. a. $33 \frac{63}{90} = 33 \frac{7}{10}$ b. $35 \frac{35}{70} = 35 \frac{1}{2}$
   c. $35 \frac{42}{60} = 35 \frac{7}{10}$ d. $95 \frac{32}{80} = 95 \frac{2}{5}$
   e. $92 \frac{35}{50} = 92 \frac{7}{10}$ f. $182 \frac{8}{40} = 182 \frac{1}{5}$
5. a. 154 r15; 154   b. 168 r32; 168
6. 10,700 ÷ 100 = 107 people

Page 36
1. a. 1,438   b. 518   c. 1,443   d. 484   e. 1,062   f. 1,035
2. a. 9,022 r5   b. 3,162   c. 5,948 r3
   d. 4,268 r1   e. 7,940 r3   f. 8,436 r3
3. a. 500 students   b. 706 gallons   c. 149,265 ft.²
4. a. 3,702   b. 6,126   c. 4,417   d. 7,218   e. 8,464   f. 5,912
5. 66 points
6. 16,896

Page 37
1. a. 24; 24, 48, 48   b. 44; 44, 44, 44
   c. 12; 14, 28, 28   d. 13; 22, 66, 66
2. a. 31 r2   b. 38 r2   c. 12   d. 10 r20
3. a. 16 r11   b. 50   c. 19 r21   d. 11 r4   e. 49   f. 5 r8
4. a. 275   b. 646   c. 365   d. 1,369
5. 15 cartons, 4 eggs left over
6. 37 bins, 9 blocks left over

Page 38
1. a. 100   b. 162.5   c. 38   d. $9   e. 10   f. 10
2. a. 85°F   b. 87°F   c. 82°F   d. 80.5°F   e. 86.5°F   f. 85.2°F
3. a. 2   b. 3   c. 1   d. 4   e. 4.5   f. 5.5
4. a. 116 marbles   b. 13.6 fruit
   c. 11 pencils   d. 81.8 matches
5. 17
6. Answers will vary.

Page 39
1. a. correct   b. 171   c. correct
   d. 293   e. 1,378   f. correct
2. a. 20   b. correct   c. 3
   d. correct   e. correct   f. correct
3. a. false   b. true   c. false
   d. true   e. true   f. false
4. a. D   b. F   c. E   d. A   e. C   f. B
5. 16 birds
6. 12 × 8 = ▲ or 12 × ▲ = 8

Page 40
1. **a.** 150 **b.** 36 **c.** 33 **d.** 16 **e.** 27 **f.** 77
2. **a.** 36 **b.** 33 **c.** 18 **d.** 10 **e.** 8 **f.** 8
3. **a.** 35 **b.** 41 **c.** 56 **d.** 80 **e.** 7 **f.** 24
4. **a.** 52 **b.** 3 **c.** 53 **d.** 197 **e.** 2 **f.** 56
5. **a.** 22 **b.** 40 **c.** 7 **d.** 1,422 **e.** 4,480 **f.** 142
6. $17 + (3 + 5) \times 4 = 16 - 7 + (8 \times 5) = 49$

Page 41
1. **a.** 3.5 **b.** 3 **c.** 1.2 **d.** 21 **e.** 1 **f.** 6
2. **a.** 11 **b.** 4 **c.** 1.4 **d.** 1.2 **e.** 8.4 **f.** 7.7
3. **a.** 28.2 **b.** 109.5 **c.** 5 **d.** 21.9 **e.** 13.5 **f.** 75

4. **a.** 7   **b.** $\frac{3}{5}$ or 0.6   **c.** 3

   d. 5   **e.** $2\frac{3}{4}$ or $\frac{11}{4}$ **f.** 45

5. **a.** 1   **b.** $2\frac{3}{5}$ **c.** 5   **d.** 10.1
6. $(0.4 + 0.3) \times 12 - 0.2 - 1.0 = 7.2$

Page 42
1. **a.** 486 **b.** 0 **c.** 574 **d.** 381 **e.** 3.4 **f.** 3,784
2. **a.** 6 **b.** 700 **c.** 5 **d.** 100 **e.** 0 **f.** 560
3. **a.** 2 **b.** 3 **c.** 99 **d.** 57 **e.** 13.4 **f.** 13
4. **a.** $M = 10 + (7 \times 3 \times 2)$ **b.** $Z = (16 + 17 + 18) \div 3$
   c. $(11 + 9) \div 4 \times 7 = K$ **d.** $H = (11 \times 12) \div 2 + 4$
5. **a.** $M = 52$ **b.** $Z = 17$ **c.** $K = 35$ **d.** $H = 70$
6. $N = ((9.8 \div 2) + 0.1) \div 8 = 0.625$ or $\frac{5}{8}$

Page 43
1. **a.** 0 **b.** 0 **c.** 0 **d.** 0 **e.** 0 **f.** 0
2. **a.** 1,689,599 **b.** 1,184,000 **c.** 11,533,000
   d. 187,000 **e.** 777,500 **f.** 61,250,000
3. **a.** 1,230,810 **b.** 4,859,400 **c.** 67,128,000
   d. 26,850 **e.** 1,526,400 **f.** 362,300
4. **a.**
```
  1 0 1 , 7 6 0
+ 3 2 8 , 3 3 7
  4 3 0 , 0 9 7
```
   b.
```
  4 , 7 1 2 , 9 9 4
- 1 , 6 6 4 , 6 8 4
  3 , 0 4 8 , 3 1 0
```
   c.
```
    1 1 8 , 6 8 0
5) 5 9 3 , 4 0 0
```
   d.
```
      3 0 7
    ×   4 7
    2 , 1 4 9
+ 1 2 , 2 8 0
  1 4 , 4 2 9
```
5. 11,352,000 bags
6. $\$460,000 - \$293,800 = \$166,200$

Page 44
1. **a.** $M = 51$ **b.** $W = 19$ **c.** $V = 10$
   d. $D = 9.2$ **e.** $K = 26$ **f.** $A = 7$
2. **a.** $B = 21$ **b.** $C = 56$ **c.** $E = 6$
   d. $T = 27$ **e.** $Z = 35$ **f.** $Y = 2$
3. **a.** $N = 3$ **b.** $H = 8$ **c.** $P = 1.5$
   d. $R = 160$ **e.** $S = 3.7$ **f.** $F = \frac{2}{6}$ or $\frac{1}{3}$

4. **a.** $\$42.50 \div 5 = G$ **b.** $G + 4 + 6 = 13$
   c. $60 \div (4 \times 3) = G$ **d.** $(5 \times 7) + (6 \times G) = 71$
5. **a.** $G = \$8.50$ **b.** $G = 3$ apples
   c. $G = 5$ trays   **d.** $G = 6$ lettuce plants
6. $20 \div (7 + 3) + 50 - 7 = (9 \times 5)$

Page 45
1. **a.** $4.75 **b.** $3.00 **c.** $81.65
   d. $100.00 **e.** $3.45 **f.** $1,010.90
2. **a.** $13.07 **b.** $14.28 **c.** $16.86
   d. $0.22 **e.** $9.46 **f.** $13.77
3. **a.** $32.00 **b.** $65.03 **c.** $39.15
   d. $2.85 **e.** $2.55 **f.** $2.39
4. **a.** $4.65 **b.** $10.55 **c.** $10.30
   d. $6.03 **e.** $1.71 **f.** $3.85
5. $(3 \times \$2.25) + (4 \times \$0.99) + (2 \times \$1.45) = \$13.61$
6. $7.74

Page 46
1. **a.** $d = 30$ **b.** $Y = 14$ **c.** $s = 9$ **d.** $T = 25$ **e.** $W = 48$ **f.** $m = 9$
2. **a.** $(5 \times 100) - (6 \times 7) = 458$ **b.** $(49 \div 7) + (8 \times 2) = 23$
   c. $(15 + 9) \times 3 \div 8 = 9$ **d.** $(11.9 + 6) - 9.3 = 8.6$
   e. $5^2 \times (4 \times 1) = 100$ **f.** $(22 \div 2) \times 12 + 8 = 140$
3. **a.** 92 **b.** 12 **c.** 12.3 **d.** 394 **e.** 129 **f.** 120
4. **a.** 4 **b.** 0.6 **c.** 10.2 **d.** 3.5 **e.** 4.3 **f.** 2.94
5. **a.** 12 **b.** 11 **c.** 10 **d.** 11
Equation c. matches the diagram (10).
6. $\$27.25 - \$25.50 =$ sales tax; tax $= \$1.75$

Page 47
1. **a.** true **b.** false **c.** true
   d. false **e.** false **f.** false
2. **a.** 77 **b.** 189 **c.** 16 **d.** 180 **e.** 6 **f.** 50
3. **a.** 782 **b.** 789 **c.** 7
   d. 3,124 **e.** 778 **f.** 146,500
4. **a.** $N \times 2 + 6 = 50$, $N = 22$
   b. $N \times 7 - 15 = 62$, $N = 11$
   c. $(N + 100) \div 5 = 40$, $N = 100$
   d. $(N - 13) \times 3 = 237$, $N = 92$
   e. $(N \div 2) - 57 = 50$, $N = 214$
   f. $(N \div 3) + 47 = 69$, $N = 66$
5. 18×1, 1×18, 9×2, 2×9, 6×3, 3×6
6. $9,872 \div 8 = 1,234$ erasers

Page 48
1. **a.** true **b.** true **c.** false **d.** false
2. **a.** 7 **b.** 4 **c.** 19 **d.** 12 **e.** 1 **f.** 13
3. **a.** false, $135 **b.** false, 23 **c.** true **d.** false, 156
4. **a.** $8 \times N = 24$, $N = 3$ **b.** $N \div 4 = 12$, $N = 48$
   c. $N - 17 = 45$, $N = 62$ **d.** $N^2 + 9 = 90$, $N = 9$
5. **a.** $\# = 3.3$ **b.** $\# = \frac{6}{4}$ or $1\frac{2}{4}$ or $1\frac{1}{2}$ **c.** $\# = 2.2$
   d. $\# = 6\frac{3}{8}$ **e.** $\# = 1.1$ **f.** $\# = 5.7$
6. Answers will vary.

Page 49
1. **a.** 81 **b.** 400 **c.** 196 **d.** 27 **e.** 1,000 **f.** 64
2. **a.** 64 **b.** 216 **c.** 49 **d.** 125 **e.** 144 **f.** 8,000
3. **a.** 1, 1 **b.** 4, 8 **c.** 9, 27
   d. 16, 64 **e.** 25, 125 **f.** 36, 216
4. **a.** $16 + 9 = 25$ **b.** $4 - 1 = 3$ **c.** $81 - 25 = 56$
   d. $16 + 25 = 41$ **e.** $144 - 64 = 80$ **f.** $49 + 1 + 9 = 59$
5. **a.** 3 **b.** 5 **c.** 7 **d.** 9 **e.** 11 **f.** 13
Pattern: increasing by two each time
6. **a.** 4096 Emerald Street
   b. September 25, 1995
   c. 729-5832

Answer Key

Page 50
1. **a.** > **b.** > **c.** > **d.** < **e.** = **f.** >
2. **a.** 46,201,500 **b.** 46,790,208
   c. 21,703 **d.** 399,999
   e. 245,296,200 **f.** 27,486,295
3. **a.** 16,428 miles and 21,428 miles
   b. 9,986 miles and 14,986 miles
   c. 51,725 miles and 56,725 miles
   d. 100,675 miles and 105,675 miles
4. Answers may vary. Check tree diagrams for accuracy.
5. **a.** 4 **b.** 7 **c.** 6
6. Factor trees may vary. $2 \times 2 \times 2 \times 3 \times 3 \times 5 \times 5 \times 5$

Page 51
1. **a.** -5, -3, -2, -1, 0, 1, 3, 4, 6
   b. -10, -5, -3, -1, 0, 1, 2, 5, 6
   c. -6, -4, -2, 0, 2, 4, 6
2. **a.** 7, 5, 3, 1, 0, -1, -3, -5
   b. 20, 10, 5, 0, -10, -15, -20, -30
   c. 19, 18, 15, 14, 13, 0, -6, -10, -13, -15
3. **a.** 89°F **b.** 80°F **c.** 83°F **d.** 95°F **e.** 78°F **f.** 74°F
4. **a.** $5 **b.** $8 **c.** $0 **d.** -$5 **e.** -$24 **f.** -$57
5. **a.** -5,
   b. 5,
   c. 7,
   d. -2
6. **a.** 3 **b.** 9 **c.** -8 **d.** 2

Page 52
1. **a.** c **b.** c **c.** p **d.** p **e.** c **f.** p
2. **a.** 16, 38, 156, 344 **b.** 21, 54, 225
   c. 40, 88, 164 **d.** 60, 95, 120
   e. 72, 90, 684 **f.** 77, 105, 196, 1,260
3. Possible answers:
   a. 73 + 5, 71 + 7, 67 + 11, 61 + 17, 59 + 19, 47 + 31, 41 + 37
   b. 19 + 5, 17 + 7, 13 + 11
   c. 97 + 3, 89 + 11, 83 + 17, 71 + 29, 59 + 41, 53 + 47
   d. 53 + 7, 47 + 13, 43 + 17, 41 + 19, 37 + 23, 31 + 29
   e. 23 + 7, 19 + 11, 17 + 13
   f. 83 + 7, 79 + 11, 73 + 17, 71 + 19, 67 + 23, 61 + 29, 59 + 31, 53 + 37, 47 + 43
4. Possible answers:
   a. 6, 8, 9, 10, 12, 14
   b. 18, 20, 21, 22
   c. 51, 52, 54, 55, 56, 57, 58
   d. 81, 82, 84, 85, 86, 87, 88, 90, 91, 92, 93, 94, 95, 96, 98, 99
   e. 116, 117, 118, 119, 120, 121, 122, 123, 124
   f. 152, 153, 154, 155, 156, 158, 159
5. 2, 3, 5, 7, 11, 13, 17, 19, 23, 29, 31, 37, 41, 43, 47
6. Answers will vary.

Page 53
1. **a.** $\frac{4}{6} = \frac{2}{3}$ **b.** $\frac{2}{4} = \frac{1}{2}$ **c.** $\frac{7}{8}$ **d.** $\frac{1}{3}$ **e.** $\frac{4}{5}$ **f.** $\frac{7}{10}$
2. **a.** $\frac{2}{6} = \frac{1}{3}$ **b.** $\frac{2}{4} = \frac{1}{2}$ **c.** $\frac{1}{8}$ **d.** $\frac{2}{3}$ **e.** $\frac{1}{5}$ **f.** $\frac{3}{10}$
3. **a.** **b.** **c.**
   d. **e.** **f.**
4. **a.** $\frac{5}{6}$ **b.** $\frac{3}{4}$ **c.** $\frac{3}{8}$ **d.** $\frac{3}{6} = \frac{1}{2}$ **e.** $\frac{7}{12}$ **f.** $\frac{8}{10} = \frac{4}{5}$
5. **a.** 3 circles should be drawn with 2 shaded.
   b. 7 squares should be drawn with 4 shaded.
   c. 9 triangles should be drawn with 2 shaded.
6. $\frac{3}{4} \times 24 = 18$ broken, 6 not broken

Page 54
1. **a.** 4 **b.** 3 **c.** 6 **d.** 2 **e.** 9 **f.** 8
2. **a.** 2 **b.** 4 **c.** 2 **d.** 4 **e.** 3 **f.** 5
3. **a.** 12 **b.** 11 **c.** 20 **d.** 75 **e.** 12 **f.** 48
4. **a.** 20 cars **b.** 10 letters
   c. 91 emails **d.** 35 minutes
5. **a.** 9 (15 objects should be drawn with 9 shaded.)
   b. 12 (18 objects should be drawn with 12 shaded.)
6. No, $\frac{4}{5} \times 90 = 72$

Page 55
1. **a.** $\frac{10}{12}$ **b.** $\frac{5}{50}$ **c.** $\frac{8}{12}$ **d.** $\frac{10}{60}$ **e.** $\frac{9}{12}$ **f.** $\frac{24}{30}$
2. **a.** $\frac{1}{2}$ **b.** $\frac{1}{2}$ **c.** $\frac{3}{4}$ **d.** $\frac{3}{5}$ **e.** $\frac{2}{3}$ **f.** $\frac{2}{4}$
3. **a.** 2 **b.** 4 **c.** 2 **d.** 2 **e.** 3 **f.** 2
4. **a.** 4 **b.** 4 **c.** 12 **d.** 25 **e.** 9 **f.** 15
5. **a.** true **b.** true **c.** false
   d. false **e.** true **f.** true
6. **a.** $\frac{12}{60}, \frac{1}{5}$ **b.** $\frac{15}{60}, \frac{1}{4}$ **c.** $\frac{9}{60}, \frac{3}{20}$
   d. $\frac{10}{60}, \frac{1}{6}$ **e.** $\frac{14}{60}, \frac{7}{30}$

Page 56
1. **a.** $\frac{3}{2}, 1\frac{1}{2}$ **b.** $\frac{7}{4}, 1\frac{3}{4}$ **c.** $\frac{12}{8}, 1\frac{1}{2}$
   d. $\frac{24}{8}, 3$ **e.** $\frac{13}{10}, 1\frac{3}{10}$ **f.** $\frac{9}{4}, 2\frac{1}{4}$
2. **a.** $1\frac{4}{5}$ **b.** $2\frac{2}{3}$ **c.** $2\frac{1}{2}$ **d.** $1\frac{3}{5}$ **e.** $1\frac{1}{3}$ **f.** $1\frac{4}{6} = 1\frac{2}{3}$
3. **a.** $\frac{5}{2}$ **b.** $\frac{7}{5}$ **c.** $\frac{7}{3}$ **d.** $\frac{23}{5}$ **e.** $\frac{21}{8}$ **f.** $\frac{22}{5}$
4. **a.** $1\frac{7}{8}$ **b.** $2\frac{1}{10}$ **c.** $3\frac{2}{3}$
   d. $1\frac{7}{10}$ **e.** $2\frac{3}{6} = 2\frac{1}{2}$ **f.** $3\frac{4}{5}$
5. Possible answers:
   a. **b.**
6. **a.** $\frac{11}{4}, \frac{16}{4}, \frac{1}{4}, \frac{14}{4}, \frac{12}{4}, \frac{10}{4}$ **b.** $\frac{1}{4}, \frac{10}{4}, 2\frac{3}{4}, 3, \frac{14}{4}, \frac{16}{4}$

Page 57

1. **a.** false   **b.** false   **c.** true
   d. true   **e.** true   **f.** true
2. **a.** $\frac{4}{10} + \frac{1}{10} = \frac{5}{10} = \frac{1}{2}$ **b.** $\frac{6}{8} + \frac{3}{8} = \frac{9}{8} = 1\frac{1}{8}$
   c. $\frac{8}{10} = \frac{4}{5}$ **d.** $\frac{5}{6}$ **e.** $\frac{9}{10}$ **f.** $\frac{7}{8}$
3. **a.** $\frac{5}{6} - \frac{2}{6} = \frac{3}{6} = \frac{1}{2}$ **b.** $\frac{7}{10} - \frac{4}{10} = \frac{3}{10}$ **c.** $\frac{3}{8}$
   d. $\frac{2}{12} = \frac{1}{6}$ **e.** $\frac{1}{4}$ **f.** $\frac{4}{10} = \frac{2}{5}$
4. **a.** $\frac{6}{5} = 1\frac{1}{5}$ **b.** $\frac{4}{3} = 1\frac{1}{3}$ **c.** $\frac{10}{12} = \frac{5}{6}$
   d. $\frac{18}{10} = 1\frac{8}{10} = 1\frac{4}{5}$ **e.** $\frac{15}{4} = 3\frac{3}{4}$ **f.** $\frac{12}{8} = 1\frac{4}{8} = 1\frac{1}{2}$
5. one-sixth, $\frac{2}{6}$, two-thirds, 1, $\frac{4}{3}$, two and one-third
6. George

Page 58

1. **a.** $\frac{10}{12} = \frac{5}{6}$ **b.** $\frac{6}{9} = \frac{2}{3}$ **c.** $\frac{6}{8} = \frac{3}{4}$
   d. $\frac{2}{4} = \frac{1}{2}$ **e.** $\frac{3}{5}$ **f.** $\frac{8}{10} = \frac{4}{5}$
2. **a.** $\frac{13}{10} = 1\frac{3}{10}$ **b.** $\frac{15}{10} = 1\frac{1}{2}$ **c.** $\frac{17}{10} = 1\frac{7}{10}$
   d. $\frac{12}{10} = 1\frac{1}{5}$ **e.** $\frac{15}{10} = 1\frac{1}{2}$ **f.** $\frac{19}{10} = 1\frac{9}{10}$
3. **a.** $\frac{7}{5} = 1\frac{2}{5}$ **b.** $\frac{14}{8} = 1\frac{6}{8} = 1\frac{3}{4}$ **c.** $\frac{6}{4} = 1\frac{1}{2}$
   d. $\frac{17}{10} = 1\frac{7}{10}$ **e.** $\frac{7}{4} = 1\frac{3}{4}$ **f.** $\frac{11}{5} = 2\frac{1}{5}$
4. **a.** $\frac{3}{12} + \frac{7}{12} = \frac{10}{12} = \frac{5}{6}$ **b.** $\frac{5}{10} + \frac{3}{10} = \frac{8}{10} = \frac{4}{5}$
   c. $\frac{1}{6} + \frac{4}{6} = \frac{5}{6}$ **d.** $\frac{3}{10} + \frac{8}{10} = \frac{11}{10} = 1\frac{1}{10}$
   e. $\frac{3}{6} + \frac{5}{6} = \frac{8}{6} = 1\frac{1}{3}$ **f.** $\frac{3}{9} + \frac{2}{9} = \frac{5}{9}$
5. $\frac{1}{8} + \frac{3}{4} = \frac{1}{8} + \frac{6}{8} = \frac{7}{8}$ of the chocolate bars
6. $(\frac{1}{4} \times 3) + \frac{1}{2} = \frac{3}{4} + \frac{1}{2} = \frac{3}{4} + \frac{2}{4} = \frac{5}{4} = 1\frac{1}{4}$ cups

Page 59

1. **a.** $\frac{2}{3}$ **b.** $\frac{2}{3}$ **c.** $\frac{3}{4}$ **d.** $\frac{7}{8}$ **e.** $\frac{1}{5}$ **f.** $\frac{1}{3}$
2. **a.** $\frac{3}{10}$ **b.** $\frac{2}{12} = \frac{1}{6}$ **c.** $\frac{2}{8} = \frac{1}{4}$
   d. $\frac{1}{6}$ **e.** $\frac{2}{4} = \frac{1}{2}$ **f.** $\frac{3}{9} = \frac{1}{3}$
3. **a.** $\frac{9}{10} - \frac{4}{10} = \frac{5}{10} = \frac{1}{2}$ **b.** $\frac{7}{8} - \frac{2}{8} = \frac{5}{8}$ **c.** $\frac{5}{6} - \frac{4}{6} = \frac{1}{6}$
   d. $\frac{8}{10} - \frac{1}{10} = \frac{7}{10}$ **e.** $\frac{7}{9} - \frac{3}{9} = \frac{4}{9}$ **f.** $\frac{10}{12} - \frac{3}{12} = \frac{7}{12}$
4. **a.** $\frac{6}{10} - \frac{4}{10} = \frac{2}{10} = \frac{1}{5}$ **b.** $\frac{7}{12} - \frac{6}{12} = \frac{1}{12}$ **c.** $\frac{6}{9} - \frac{4}{9} = \frac{2}{9}$
   d. $\frac{8}{10} - \frac{4}{10} = \frac{4}{10} = \frac{2}{5}$ **e.** $\frac{3}{8} - \frac{2}{8} = \frac{1}{8}$ **f.** $\frac{4}{6} - \frac{3}{6} = \frac{1}{6}$
5. $\frac{5}{8} - \frac{1}{2} = \frac{5}{8} - \frac{4}{8} = \frac{1}{8}$
6. $\frac{1}{5}$ left

Page 60

1. **a.** $\frac{16}{10}$ **b.** $\frac{9}{4}$ **c.** $\frac{11}{3}$ **d.** $\frac{37}{8}$ **e.** $\frac{15}{2}$ **f.** $\frac{14}{5}$
2. **a.** $1\frac{1}{3}$ **b.** $1\frac{2}{5}$ **c.** $2\frac{1}{10}$ **d.** 2   **e.** $2\frac{1}{8}$ **f.** $2\frac{2}{6} = 2\frac{1}{3}$
3. **a.** $\frac{1}{4} + \frac{2}{4} = \frac{3}{4}$ **b.** $\frac{4}{6} + \frac{4}{6} = \frac{8}{6} = 1\frac{1}{3}$
   c. $\frac{3}{8} + \frac{2}{8} = \frac{5}{8}$ **d.** $\frac{7}{10} + \frac{4}{10} = \frac{11}{10} = 1\frac{1}{10}$
   e. $\frac{1}{9} + \frac{6}{9} = \frac{7}{9}$ **f.** $\frac{4}{12} + \frac{5}{12} = \frac{9}{12} = \frac{3}{4}$
4. **a.** $\frac{5}{8} - \frac{2}{8} = \frac{3}{8}$ **b.** $\frac{9}{10} - \frac{8}{10} = \frac{1}{10}$
   c. $\frac{5}{6} - \frac{4}{6} = \frac{1}{6}$ **d.** $\frac{11}{12} - \frac{9}{12} = \frac{2}{12} = \frac{1}{6}$
   e. $\frac{8}{10} - \frac{5}{10} = \frac{3}{10}$ **f.** $\frac{7}{9} - \frac{6}{9} = \frac{1}{9}$
5. $\frac{3}{4} + \frac{5}{8} = \frac{6}{8} + \frac{5}{8} = \frac{11}{8} = 1\frac{3}{8}$ fruits
6. Word problems will vary. $\frac{7}{8} - \frac{1}{2} = \frac{7}{8} - \frac{4}{8} = \frac{3}{8}$

Page 61

1. **a.** 9   **b.** 32   **c.** 5   **d.** 23   **e.** 21   **f.** 73
2. **a.** $\frac{3}{4} + \frac{3}{4}; \frac{6}{4}; 1\frac{1}{2}$ **b.** $\frac{1}{4} + \frac{1}{4} + \frac{1}{4}; \frac{3}{4}; \frac{3}{4}$
   c. $\frac{2}{3} + \frac{2}{3} + \frac{2}{3} + \frac{2}{3}; \frac{8}{3}; 2\frac{2}{3}$ **d.** $\frac{3}{5} + \frac{3}{5} + \frac{3}{5}; \frac{9}{5}; 1\frac{4}{5}$
   e. $\frac{6}{8} + \frac{6}{8}; \frac{12}{8}; 1\frac{1}{2}$ **f.** $\frac{2}{10} + \frac{2}{10} + \frac{2}{10} + \frac{2}{10}; \frac{8}{10}; \frac{4}{5}$
3. **a.** $6   **b.** $40   **c.** 1.5 ft.   **d.** 3,000 gal.
4. **a.** $\frac{9}{8} = 1\frac{1}{8}$ **b.** $\frac{6}{10} = \frac{3}{5}$ **c.** $\frac{10}{5} = 2$
   d. $\frac{8}{3} = 2\frac{2}{3}$ **e.** $\frac{18}{4} = 4\frac{1}{2}$ **f.** $\frac{45}{6} = 7\frac{1}{2}$
5. **a.** $\frac{2}{12} = \frac{1}{6}$ **b.** $\frac{20}{30} = \frac{2}{3}$ **c.** $\frac{10}{40} = \frac{1}{4}$
   d. $\frac{6}{32} = \frac{3}{16}$ **e.** $\frac{9}{20}$ **f.** $\frac{8}{30} = \frac{4}{15}$
6. **a.** 8   **b.** 18   **c.** 18

Page 62

1. **a.**

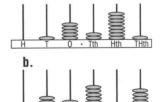

   b.

   c.

2. **a.** 9.6   **b.** 9.27   **c.** 19.014
   d. 90.052   **e.** 90.002   **f.** 19.20
3. **a.** 7 hundredths   **b.** 7 thousandths   **c.** 7 ones
   d. 7 ones   **e.** 7 hundredths   **f.** 7 tenths
4. **a.** 0.22   **b.** 0.19   **c.** 0.4   **d.** 0.236   **e.** 0.04   **f.** 0.143
5. **a.** four and six hundred three thousandths
   b. seven and eight thousandths
   c. eleven and fifty-two hundredths
6. 3.267

Answer Key

Page 63
1. a. 7.84   b. 12.16   c. 13.77
   d. 10.705   e. 7.137   f. 16.053
2. a. 14.41   b. 14.91
   c. 14.89   d. 65.441
3. a. $99.30   b. $107.10   c. $117.05
   d. $61.40   e. $176.85   f. $197.15
4. a. $311.51   b. $251.32   c. $370.97   d. $552.55
5. 12.101 pounds
6. Word problems will vary. 4.29 + 3.60 + 15 = 22.89 miles

Page 64
1. a. 0.2   b. 1.1   c. 1.02   d. 2.13   e. 3.3   f. 4.87
2. a. 0.64   b. 4.77   c. 20.88   d. 2.575   e. 2.522   f. 3.459
3. a. $6.15   b. $85.53   c. $155.73
   d. $236.58   e. $81.50   f. $36.53
4. a. 57.78   b. 0.93   c. 4.595   d. 4.674   e. 8.57   f. 3.649
5. 3.92 ft.
6. Word problems will vary. $16.30 − $12.49 = $3.81

Page 65
1. a. 13.83   b. 15.96   c. 19.52
   d. 4.611   e. 12.430   f. 153.712
2. a. $8.25   b. $20.50   c. $12.30
   d. $12.91   e. $9.89   f. $18.77
3. a. $41.70   b. $21.81   c. $103.30
   d. $91.60   e. $1,202.31   f. $1,286.60
4. a. 7.56 ft.   b. 5.25 ft.   c. 74.25 ft.
   d. 76.45 ft.   e. 264.95 ft.   f. 50.52 ft.
5. 173.25 minutes (2 hours and 53.25 min.)
6. 1 gallon of milk for $2.50

Page 66
1. a. 3.43   b. 4.31   c. 6.4   d. 9.21   e. 3.064   f. 4.341
2. a. 8.1   b. 5.4   c. 4.05   d. 3.24   e. 2.7   f. 1.8
3. a. $9.28   b. $5.34   c. $11.25
   d. $6.12   e. $12.11   f. $7.23
4. a. $1.23   b. $0.87   c. $0.67   d. $0.75   e. $0.78   f. $0.33
5. a. 5.04   b. 2.025   c. $13.07   d. $0.78
6. No, correct answer = 12.49

Page 67
1. a. 4.36   b. 21.76   c. 61.73   d. 9   e. 463.5   f. 0.71
2. a. 631   b. 47.2   c. 8,179
   d. 6,421   e. 110,421   f. 26,500
3. a. 0.0452   b. 0.671   c. 1.296
   d. 13.021   e. 42.1639   f. 21.4853
4. a. 0.00421   b. 6.973   c. 0.0491
   d. 0.32101   e. 1.04985   f. 0.024691
5. a. 46,830; 4,683; 468.3; 46.83; 4.683; 0.4683
   b. 924,100; 92,410; 9,241; 924.10; 92.41; 9.241
   c. 4,630; 463; 46.3; 4.63; 0.463; 0.0463
   d. 10,480; 1,048; 104.8; 10.48; 1.048; 0.1048
   e. 110,216; 11,021.6; 1,102.16; 110.216; 11.0216;
      1.10216
   f. 30,050; 3,005; 300.5; 30.05; 3.005; 0.3005
6. a. move the decimal one place to the right
   b. move the decimal two places to the right
   c. move the decimal three places to the right
   d. move the decimal one place to the left
   e. move the decimal two places to the left

Page 68
1. a. 25.72   b. 9.18   c. 24.77
   d. 15.911   e. 14.805   f. 167.426
2. a. $2.89   b. $4.27   c. $2.19   d. $2.89   e. $5.88   f. $22.11
3. a. 19.2 lb.   b. 33.6 lb.   c. 21.38 lb.
   d. 1.25 lb.   e. 2.25 lb.   f. 214 lb.
4. a. 1.229   b. 4.932   c. 8.08   d. 3.499   e. 4.921   f. 3.635
5. a. 197.956   b. $5.52   c. 31.32   d. 7.6655
6. 21.49 ft.

Page 69
1. a. 0.63   b. 0.246   c. 0.8   d. 0.09   e. 0.042   f. 0.6
2. a. $\frac{2}{10}$ b. $\frac{85}{100}$ c. $\frac{326}{1,000}$ d. $\frac{4}{100}$ e. $\frac{406}{1,000}$ f. $\frac{1}{1,000}$
3. a. $\frac{1}{5} = \frac{2}{10} = 0.2$ b. $\frac{1}{20} = \frac{5}{100} = 0.05$
   c. $\frac{3}{4} = \frac{75}{100} = 0.75$ d. $\frac{1}{8} = \frac{125}{1,000} = 0.125$
   e. $\frac{3}{5} = \frac{60}{100} = 0.6$ f. $\frac{3}{8} = \frac{375}{1,000} = 0.375$
4. a. $\frac{19}{100}$, 0.19   b. $\frac{25}{100}$, 0.25   c. $\frac{80}{100}$, 0.8
   d. $\frac{52}{100}$, 0.52   e. $\frac{73}{100}$, 0.73   f. $\frac{5}{100}$, 0.05
5. a. $\frac{44}{100} = 0.44$ b. $0.123 = \frac{123}{1,000}$
6.

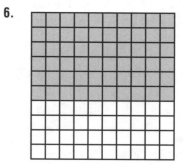

Page 70
1. a. 6.2   b. 4.7   c. 1.1   d. 143.5   e. 28.0   f. 18.0
2. a. 6.49   b. 8.02   c. 7.40   d. 211.09   e. 42.12   f. 879.64
3. a. 10 + 3 + 106 = 119   b. 2 + 4 + 19 = 25
   c. 903 + 19 + 15 = 937   d. 7 + 9 + 4 = 20
   e. 421 + 1 + 5 = 427   f. 13 + 3 + 19 = 35
4. a. 17.478, 17.5   b. 49.967, 50.0
   c. 99.879, 99.9   d. 144.19, 144.2
   e. 413.164, 413.2   f. 424.265, 424.3
5. a. $4 + $3 + $4 + $3 + $4 = $18
   b. No, actual cost = $18.05
6. $3.85 ÷ 2 = $1.925, rounded = $1.93

Page 71
1. a. 20%   b. 90%   c. 60%   d. 81%   e. 36%   f. 2%
2. a. 0.3, 30%   b. 0.9, 90%   c. 0.41, 41%
   d. 0.73, 73%   e. 0.27, 27%   f. 0.14, 14%
3. a. 61%   b. 26%   c. $\frac{41}{100}$ d. 90%   e. 50%   f. 0.77
4. a. $\frac{1}{2} = 50\%$ b. $\frac{1}{4} = 25\%$ c. $\frac{1}{20} = 5\%$
   d. $\frac{1}{5} = 20\%$ e. $\frac{3}{4} = 75\%$ f. $\frac{1}{10} = 10\%$

5. a. 25% = 30

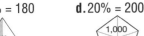

b. 25% = 125

c. 50% = 180

d. 20% = 200

6. a. $2, $18 **b.** $25, $25 **c.** $6, $24
d. $20, $60 **e.** $45, $855 **f.** $24, $96

Page 72
1. a. 30% **b.** 70% **c.** 1% **d.** 12% **e.** 56% **f.** 130%
2. a. 0.07 **b.** 0.03 **c.** 0.4 **d.** 0.59 **e.** 0.63 **f.** 1.21
3. a. 40% **b.** 80% **c.** 8% **d.** 90% **e.** 47% **f.** 136%
4. a. $\frac{89}{100}$ **b.** 34% **c.** 0.5

5. a. 98% **b.** $\frac{120}{100}$ **c.** 750%

6. a. $\frac{20}{100} = \frac{1}{5}$ **b.** $\frac{16}{100} = \frac{4}{25}$ **c.** $\frac{140}{100} = 1\frac{2}{5}$ **d.** $\frac{290}{100} = 2\frac{9}{10}$

Page 73
1. a. 1 $10 bill, 1 $1 bill, 3 quarters, 1 nickel
 b. 1 $20 bill, 1 $5 bill, 2 $1 bills (or 1 $2 bill), 1 dime, 1 nickel
 c. 2 $20 bills, 3 $1 bills (or 1 $2 bill and 1 $1 bill), 3 quarters, 2 dimes
 d. 1 $100 bill, 1 $20 bill, 1 $5 bill, 1 $1 bill, 1 quarter, 2 dimes
2. a. $16.60 **b.** $22.15 **c.** $5.85
 d. $28.10 **e.** $32.95 **f.** $13.20
3. a. $7.00 **b.** $19.40
4. a. $15.02, $15.00 **b.** $24.85, $24.85
 c. $16.68, $16.70 **d.** $12.29, $12.30
5. a. $11.80 **b.** No, total = $20.30
6. a. a bag of 15 oranges for $2.55 **b.** $6.95

Page 74
1. a. 1 **b.** 4 **c.** 2 **d.** 2 **e.** 4 **f.** 5

2. a.   **b.** **c.**

d.   **e.** **f.**

3. a.   **b.**   **c.**

d.   **e.** **f.**

4. a.   **b.** Drawings will vary.

5. A, B, C, D, E, H, I, K, M, O, T, U, V, W, X, Y
6.

Page 75
1. a. yes **b.** no **c.** no **d.** yes **e.** no **f.** yes
2. a. 3 **b.** 2 **c.** 4 **d.** 5 **e.** 6 **f.** 8
3. a. yes **b.** yes **c.** yes **d.** yes **e.** no **f.** no

4. a.   **b.**   **c.**

d.   **e.**   **f.**

5.
6. yes, 3

Page 76
1. a., e., and f. are perpendicular lines
2. a. true **b.** false **c.** true **d.** true **e.** false **f.** true

3. a.   **b.**   **c.**

d.   **e.**   **f.**

4. a. 4, 2 **b.** 4, 2 **c.** 5, 5 **d.** 6, 9 **e.** 7, 14 **f.** 8, 20
5. 4 and 5
6. E, F, H, I, L, T

Page 77
1. a., b., and c. are parallel lines
2. a. vertical **b.** horizontal **c.** horizontal
 d. vertical **e.** neither **f.** neither
3. a. true **b.** false **c.** true **d.** false **e.** true **f.** false
4. b., c., d., and e. have parallel lines (H, E, F, N)
5. C, J, O, Q, S, V, X (U can be considered.)
6. a. no,   **b.** yes,

Page 78
1. a. 50° **b.** 40° **c.** 85° **d.** 115° **e.** 120° **f.** 165°
2. a. 160° **b.** 90° **c.** 135° **d.** 180° **e.** 25° **f.** 70°
3. Angles a., c., and e. are acute.
4. Angles c. and d. are obtuse. (Angle b. is straight. Angle f. is reflex.)
5. Angles b., c., and e. are right.
6. 150°

Page 79
1. a. reflex **b.** reflex **c.** neither
 d. straight **e.** neither **f.** straight
2. Estimates will vary.
 a. 30° **b.** 90° **c.** 120° **d.** 15° **e.** 135° **f.** 175°
3. a. acute **b.** right **c.** straight
 d. obtuse **e.** obtuse **f.** reflex
4. Estimates will vary.
 a. 30° **b.** 50° **c.** 60° **d.** 120° **e.** 80° **f.** 150°
5. a. smaller = 50°, reflex = 310°
 b. smaller = 80°, reflex = 280°
 c. smaller = 15°, reflex = 345°
 d. smaller = 120°, reflex = 240°
6. All angles are the same, measuring 108°.

Page 80

1. **a.** 50° **b.** 85° **c.** 115° **d.** 135°

2. Drawings will vary. Check drawings for accuracy.

3. **a.** 15° **b.** 100° **c.** 60°

4. **a.** 310° **b.** 275° **c.** 190°

5. Drawings will vary. Check angle measurements for accuracy.

6.

Page 81

1. **a.** 90° **b.** 64° **c.** 26° **d.** 60° **e.** 60° **f.** 60°
2. **a.** right **b.** acute **c.** acute
   d. acute **e.** 180° **f.** 180°
3. **a.** 90° **b.** 60° **c.** 30° **d.** 50° **e.** 40° **f.** 45°
4. **a.** equilateral **b.** isosceles **c.** right
   d. right **e.** isosceles **f.** scalene
5. **a.** false **b.** true
6. Check drawings for accuracy. Possible drawing:

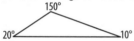

150°
20° 10°

Page 82

1. **a.** rectangular prism **b.** pentagonal prism
   c. hexagonal pyramid **d.** triangular prism
   e. triangular pyramid **f.** cube
2. **a.** cylinder **b.** cone
   c. triangular prism **d.** hexagonal prism
   e. square pyramid **f.** rectangular pyramid
3. **a.** triangular pyramid or prism (e. or d.)
   b. cube (f.)
   c. pentagonal prism (b.)
   d. rectangular prism (a.)
   e. triangular prism or pyramid (d. or e.)
   f. hexagonal pyramid (c.)
4. **a.** 6, 12, 8 **b.** 6, 12, 8 **c.** 5, 9, 6
   d. 8, 18, 12 **e.** 5, 8, 5 **f.** 4, 6, 4
5. cylinder
6. square pyramid

Page 83

1. **a.** 6 rectangles **b.** 1 square, 4 triangles
   c. 6 squares **d.** 1 rectangle, 4 triangles
   e. 2 triangles, 3 rectangles **f.** 2 hexagons, 6 rectangles

2. **a.** **b.** **c.**

   d. **e.** **f.**

3. Check drawings for accuracy.
   Should duplicate given images.
4. **a.** octagonal prism **b.** triangular pyramid
   c. square prism **d.** hexagonal pyramid

5. Answers will vary. Possible answers:
   a. cube, rectangular prism, square prism, triangular prism, square pyramid, triangular pyramid, rectangular pyramid, pentagonal pyramid, hexagonal pyramid, cylinder, cone, sphere
   b. cube, rectangular prism, square prism, triangular prism, triangular pyramid, pentagonal pyramid

6.

Page 84

1. **a.** cube, 6, 12, 8, 0, square
   b. cone, 2, 1, 1, 1, triangle
   c. cylinder, 3, 2, 0, 1, rectangle
   d. triangular pyramid, 4, 6, 4, 0, triangle
2. **a.** cone, cylinder **b.** cone
   c. cylinder **d.** cone, triangular pyramid
   e. cube **f.** triangular pyramid
3. **a.** cylinder **b.** cube
   c. rectangular prism **d.** triangular prism
4. **a.** 9 **b.** 24 **c.** 5 **d.** 4
5. triangular prism
6. Answers will vary.

Page 85

1. **a.** cylinder **b.** cone **c.** sphere
   d. cylinder **e.** cone **f.** cylinder
2. **a.** triangle, 1, 2, 1, 1, yes **b.** rectangle, 2, 3, 0, 1, yes
   c. circle, 0, 1, 0, 1, yes **d.** square, 12, 6, 8, 0, no
3. **a.** sphere **b.** in a circle
   c. in a straight line **d.** sphere
   e. cone **f.** cylinder, cone, sphere

4. **a.** **b.**

5. **a.** sphere **b.** cylinder **c.** cylinder
   d. cone **e.** sphere **f.** cone
6. cylinders; Check drawings for accuracy.

Page 86

1. **a.** , 12, 8, 6 **b.** , 2, 0, 3 **c.** , 1, 1, 2
   d. , 0, 0, 1 **e.** , 9, 6, 5
   f. , 12, 8, 6

2. **a.** **b.** **c.**
   d. **e.** or **f.**

3. **a.** triangular pyramid **b.** rectangular prism
   c. hexagonal prism **d.** triangular prism
   e. pentagonal prism **f.** square pyramid
4. b. and d. make up an open cube
5. octagonal prism
6.

Answer Key

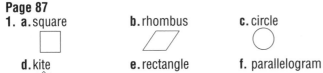

Page 87

1. **a.** square   **b.** rhombus   **c.** circle

   d. kite   **e.** rectangle   **f.** parallelogram

2. a., b., and e. are parallelograms
3. e. and f. are rhombuses
4. **a.**   **b.**   **c.**   **d.**

5. trapezoid
6. Drawings will vary. Check drawings for accuracy.

Page 88

1. **a.** 6   **b.** 9   **c.** 12   **d.** 15   **e.** 18   **f.** 21
2. **a.** 5   **b.** 10   **c.** 20   **d.** 25   **e.** 30   **f.** 35
3. **a.** 8   **b.** 16   **c.** 24   **d.** 32   **e.** 48   **f.** 56

4. **a.** △, △, ○, ○, □, □, △, △, ○, ○, □, □

   b.

   c.

   d.

5. **a.** number of triangles × 3
   b. number of pentagons × 5
   c. number of octagons × 8
6. rotate 90° clockwise around the dot

Page 89

1. **a.** center   **b.** radius   **c.** diameter

   d. circumference   **e.** arc   **f.** sector

2. **a.** center—the point in the middle
   b. semicircle—half of the inside of the circle
   c. concentric circles—circles with a common center
   d. circumference—the perimeter of the circle
   e. arc—part of the circumference
   f. sector—an area bound by two radii and an arc
3. **a.** 3 cm   **b.** 2 cm   **c.** 1.5 cm   **d.** 2.5 cm   **e.** 1 cm   **f.** 0.5 cm
4. **a.** 0.5 cm   **b.** 1.25 cm   **c.** 0.75 cm   **d.** 1 cm
5. Answers will vary.
6. Check circle drawings for accuracy.
   a. diameter should equal 2.5 in.
   b. radius should equal 1 in.

Page 90

1. **a.** 6 miles   **b.** 9 miles   **c.** 5 miles   **d.** 8 miles
2. **a.** 32 miles   **b.** 60 miles   **c.** 68 miles   **d.** 56 miles
3. **a.** 14 mm   **b.** 3 mm   **c.** 2 mm   **d.** 7 mm   **e.** 1.5 mm   **f.** 1 mm
4. **a.** 10 in., 6 in.   **b.** 10 in., 7.5 in.   **c.** 5 in., 2 in.
   d. 9 in., 5 in.   **e.** 15 in., 9 in.   **f.** 7 in., 6 in.
5. 6 miles
6. Triangle drawing should have side lengths of 3 cm, 3 cm, and 4.5 cm.

Page 91

1. **a.** yes   **b.** no   **c.** no   **d.** yes   **e.** yes   **f.** no
2. **a.**   **b.**   **c.**

   d.   **e.**   **f.**

3. **a.**   **b.**   **c.**

   d.   **e.**   **f.**

4. **a.**   **b.**   **c.**

   d.   **e.**   **f.**

5. Tessellations will vary.
6. Answers will vary.
   Sample answer: gives

Page 92

1. **a.** NE   **b.** NW   **c.** E or W   **d.** SE   **e.** SW   **f.** N or S
2. **a.** W   **b.** E   **c.** S   **d.** N   **e.** NW   **f.** NE
3. **a.** rectangle   **b.** square   **c.** circle
   d. square   **e.** rectangle   **f.** triangle
4. **a.** 15 in. W and 10 in. S   **b.** 8 in. S and 2 in. E
   c. 10 in. N and 35 in. E   **d.** 6 in. S
5. **a.** go east 1 space, then south 2 spaces
   b. go west 1 space, then south 1 space
6. **a.** 90°   **b.** 90°   **c.** 180°

Page 93

1. **a.** Banana Beach   **b.** Sultana Slide
   c. Apple Point   **d.** Cherry Cove
   e. Orange Obstacle Course   **f.** Strawberry Summit
2. **a.** 1,000 yd.   **b.** 400 yd.   **c.** 800 yd.   **d.** 800 yd.
3. **a.** SW   **b.** SE   **c.** N or NW   **d.** W   **e.** S or SE   **f.** SE
4. **a.** C7   **b.** E5   **c.** C3   **d.** E0   **e.** I2   **f.** G5
5.

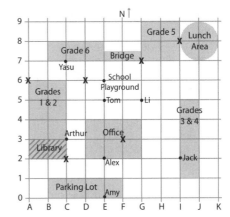

6. **a.** 150 ft.   **b.** 300 ft.   **c.** 0 ft.
   d. 300 ft.   **e.** 150 ft.   **f.** 900 ft.

Answer Key

Page 94

1.–5.

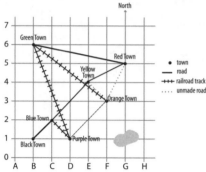

North

Green Town
Red Town
Yellow Town
Orange Town
Blue Town
Black Town
Purple Town

● town
— road
+++ railroad track
.... unmade road

6. a. N   **b.** SW   **c.** NW

Page 95

1. **a.** Nebraska   **b.** New Mexico   **c.** Nevada
2. **a.** L6   **b.** B8   **c.** O5
3. **a.** N   **b.** E   **c.** N   **d.** N
4. **a.** Oregon   **b.** Wisconsin   **c.** Mississippi
   d. Tennessee
5. **a.** North Dakota   **b.** Minnesota   **c.** Georgia
6. California (start), Arizona, New Mexico, Texas, Louisiana (finish)

Page 96

1. **a.**   **b.**   **c.**
   d.   **e.**   **f.**
2. **a.**   **b.**   **c.**
   d.   **e.**   **f.**
3. **a.** three twenty-five, or twenty-five past three
   b. seven fifty, or ten to eight
   c. ten thirty-five, or twenty-five to eleven
   d. two twenty, or twenty past two
4. **a.** 4 hours 15 min.   **b.** 5 hours 55 min.
   c. 1 hour 40 min.   **d.** 10 hours 30 min.
5. 3:10
6. Check times for accuracy.

Page 97

1. **a.** 9:22   **b.** 5:49   **c.** 4:56   **d.** 2:17   **e.** 1:34   **f.** 8:37
2. **a.** morning   **b.** morning   **c.** evening
   d. morning   **e.** morning   **f.** afternoon
3. **a.** 6:58 a.m.   **b.** 7:10 p.m.   **c.** 3:16 p.m.
   d. 2:11 a.m.   **e.** 1:23 p.m.   **f.** 1:06 a.m.

4. **a.** 3 hours 29 min.   **b.** 1 hour 27 min.
   c. 2 hours 47 min.   **d.** 5 hours 32 min.
   e. 3 hours 57 min.   **f.** 6 hours 47 min.
5. **a.** 11:49 p.m., 12:00 p.m., 1:37 a.m.
   b. 6:32 p.m., 6:30 p.m., 6:31 a.m.
   c. 10:25 p.m., 9:14 a.m., 12:01 a.m.
6. Answers will vary. Check times for accuracy.

Page 98

1. **a.** seven fifteen, or quarter past seven
   b. three twenty-seven, or twenty-seven past three
   c. nine forty-two, or eighteen to ten
   d. twelve o'five, or five past twelve
2. **a.**   **b.**   **c.**
   d.   **e.**   **f.**
3. **a.** 8:23   **b.** 2:21   **c.** 3:18   **d.** 7:02   **e.** 10:55   **f.** 10:36
4. **a.** 12:45   **b.** 4:27   **c.** 9:42   **d.** 11:54   **e.** 6:15   **f.** 4:41
5. **a.** 4 hours 12 min.   **b.** 6 hours 36 min.
   c. 10 hours 12 min.
6. **a.** 4:30 p.m.   **b.** 12:56 p.m.   **c.** 12:41 p.m.

Page 99

1. **a.** 6 minutes, 24.14 seconds
   b. 13 minutes, 36.40 seconds
   c. 6.29 seconds
   d. 1 minute, 43.05 seconds
   e. 25 minutes, 13.19 seconds
   f. 47 minutes, 12.63 seconds
2. **a.** 00:09:60   **b.** 03:26:71   **c.** 11:40:42
3. **a.** 35:25:40   **b.** 44:20:29   **c.** 26:35:10
4. **a.** 0.06 sec.   **b.** 0.11 sec.   **c.** 1.85 sec.
   d. 9.03 sec.   **e.** 1 min. 8.02 sec.   **f.** 1.14 sec.
5. **a.** 270   **b.** 4,500   **c.** 6   **d.** 5   **e.** 60   **f.** 234
6. 36 hours, 2,160 minutes, 129,600 seconds

Page 100

1.

		a			b	c	d	e	f
Aug.	Sep.	Oct.	Nov.	Dec.	Jan.		Feb.	Mar.	Apr.
		2004					**2005**		

2. **a.** 16 days   **b.** 28 days   **c.** 64 days

3.

```
                    d            f    e           c      a
        b           started      broke went to   joined went to
        born        school       arm   China     basketball camp
                                                  team
        ↓           ↓            ↓    ↓           ↓      ↓
   1995 1996 1997 1998 1999 2000 2001 2002 2003 2004 2005 2006 2007
```

4. **a.** 11:17 a.m.
   b. 1:55 p.m.
   c. 11:07 a.m. and 11:32 a.m.
   d. 11:00 a.m. and 11:25 a.m.
   e. 12:31 p.m., 1:26 p.m., and 1:51 p.m.
   f. 12:00 p.m., 12:55 p.m., and 1:20 p.m.
5. **a.** 2   **b.** 3   **c.** 5:30 p.m.
   d. 10:30 a.m.   **e.** 8:30 p.m.   **f.** 1:30 p.m.
6. **a.** 3:21 p.m.   **b.** 2 hours

Answer Key

Page 101
1. **a.** 10 a.m.　**b.** 4 p.m.　**c.** 8 p.m.
　d. 6 a.m.　**e.** 2 a.m.　**f.** 6 p.m.
2. **a.** 9 p.m.　**b.** 1 p.m.　**c.** 11 a.m.
　d. 3 p.m.　**e.** 5 a.m. (next day)
　f. 1 a.m. (next day)
3. **a.** 8:40 p.m.　**b.** 4:40 p.m.　**c.** 11:20 a.m.　**d.** 3:20 a.m.
4. **a.** 10:40 a.m.　**b.** 5:20 p.m.　**c.** 4:00 p.m.　**d.** 4:00 a.m.
5. Answers will vary.
6. Answers will vary.

Page 102
1. **a.** 50 mph　**b.** 100 mph　**c.** 80 mph
　d. 90 mph　**e.** 65 mph　**f.** 45 mph
2. **a.** 560 miles　**b.** 375 miles　**c.** 175 miles
　d. 20 miles　**e.** 70 miles　**f.** 66 miles
3. **a.** 2 hours　**b.** 2.5 hours　**c.** 10 hours　**d.** 30 min.
4. **a.** 30 mph　**b.** 2 hours　**c.** 6 mph　**d.** 240 miles
5. 665 mi. ÷ 9.5 hrs. = 70 mph
6. 3 minutes

Page 103
1. **a.** in.　**b.** ft.　**c.** ft.　**d.** in.　**e.** mi.　**f.** ft.
2. **a.** 0.5 ft.　**b.** 2.0 ft.　**c.** 1.5 ft.　**d.** 3.5 ft.　**e.** 1.75 ft.　**f.** 1.25 ft.
3. **a.** 24 in.　**b.** 36 in.　**c.** 18 in.　**d.** 33 in.　**e.** 30 in.　**f.** 36 in.
4. **a.** $1\frac{1}{3}$ yd.　**b.** $1\frac{2}{3}$ yd.　**c.** $\frac{2}{3}$ yd.　**d.** $\frac{1}{4}$ yd.　**e.** $\frac{1}{2}$ yd.　**f.** $\frac{3}{4}$ yd.
5. **a.** 8 laps　**b.** 4 laps　**c.** 20 laps
　d. 16 laps　**e.** 4 laps　**f.** 2 laps
6. Answers will vary.

Page 104
1. **a.** 4.6 cm　**b.** 3.9 cm　**c.** 8.1 cm
　d. 12 cm　**e.** 14.6 cm　**f.** 27.6 cm
2. **a.** 4.61 m　**b.** 7.38 m　**c.** 9.26 m
　d. 12.84 m　**e.** 36.95 m　**f.** 21 m
3. **a.** 1.376 km　**b.** 4.218 km　**c.** 5.798 km
　d. 6.635 km　**e.** 9.801 km　**f.** 10.635 km
4. **a.** 5,500　**b.** 115　**c.** 5.2
　d. 9.24　**e.** 4,700　**f.** 25
5. **a.** 600 mm, 60 cm　　**b.** 4.6 cm, 0.046 m
　c. 830 mm, 0.83 m　　**d.** 42 mm, 4.2 cm
　e. 1.9 cm, 0.019 m　　**f.** 241 mm, 0.241 m
6. **a.** 4,800 m　　**b.** 4.8 km

Page 105
1. **a.** 12 cm　**b.** 20 in.　**c.** 12 ft.　**d.** 18 ft.　**e.** 20 cm　**f.** 18 in.
2. **a.** 14 in.　**b.** 32 cm　**c.** 40 ft.　**d.** 19 cm　**e.** 40 in.　**f.** 70 in.
3. **a.** 28.8 cm　**b.** 57 ft.　**c.** 30 in.
　d. 66 in.　**e.** 112 ft.　**f.** 120 cm
4. **a.** 24 in.　**b.** 40 ft.　**c.** 21 in.　**d.** 24 ft.　**e.** 33 cm　**f.** 30 ft.
5. **a.** 5 cm　**b.** 4 in.　**c.** 16 ft.　**d.** 25 in.　**e.** 36 cm　**f.** 24 ft.
6. **a.** regular polygons (all sides in shape are equal length)
　b. Drawings and labels will vary. (2 of the 3 side lengths must be labeled equally, e.g., 10 in., 10 in., and 20 in.)

Page 106
1. **a.** 4, 4, 16　**b.** 6, 2, 12　**c.** 7, 3, 21
　d. 5, 5, 25　**e.** 2, 1, 2　**f.** 12, 5, 60
2. **a.** 99 ft.²　**b.** 32 cm²　**c.** 40 in.²
　d. 108 cm²　**e.** 1.5 ft.²　**f.** 81 in.²
3. **a.** 30 ft.²　**b.** 40 ft.²　**c.** 54 ft.²　**d.** 8 ft.²　**e.** 21 ft.²　**f.** 99 ft.²

4. **a.** 12 cm²　**b.** 18 cm²　**c.** 150 cm²
　d. 80 cm²　**e.** 5,000 cm²　**f.** 180 cm²

5. **a.** 34 in.²　**b.** 21 ft.²　**c.** 48 in.²
6. Possible answers: (1 in. x 42 in.), (2 in. x 21 in.), (3 in. x 14 in.), (6 in. x 7 in.)

Page 107
1. **a.** 20 in.², 10 in.²　　**b.** 28 in.², 14 in.²
　c. 24 in.², 12 in.²　　**d.** 64 in.², 32 in.²
　e. 90 in.², 45 in.²　　**f.** 12 in.², 6 in.²
2. **a.** 21 ft.²　**b.** 18 ft.²　**c.** 30 ft.²　**d.** 6 ft.²　**e.** 25 ft.²　**f.** 18 ft.²
3. **a.** 3, 9　**b.** 2, 14　**c.** 4, 36　**d.** 5, 30　**e.** 6, 60　**f.** 10, 40
4. **a.** 24 cm²　**b.** 24.5 ft.²　**c.** 9 in.²
　d. 15 ft.²　**e.** 50 in.²　**f.** 10 cm²
5. **a.** 27 in.²　**b.** 16 in.²　**c.** 100 in.²
　d. 10 ft.²　**e.** 72 ft.²　**f.** 70 ft.²
6. 120 cm²

Page 108
1. **a.** pounds　**b.** tons　**c.** pounds
　d. ounces　**e.** tons　**f.** ounces
2. **a.** 4.5 lb.　**b.** 8.25 lb.　**c.** 10.0 lb.
　d. 5.75 lb.　**e.** 7.0 lb.　**f.** 4.0 lb.
3. **a.** 96 oz.　**b.** 92 oz.　**c.** 72 oz.　**d.** 36 oz.　**e.** 163 oz.　**f.** 184 oz.
4. **a.** 7 lb. 4 oz.　**b.** 8 lb. 0 oz.　**c.** 9 lb. 8 oz.
　d. 12 lb. 12 oz.　**e.** 10 lb. 5 oz.　**f.** 5 lb. 7 oz.
5. **a.** 4,000 lb.　**b.** 18,000 lb.　**c.** 9,000 lb.
　d. 23,500 lb.　**e.** 30,500 lb.　**f.** 41,400 lb.
6. 1 T 1,630 lb.

Page 109
1. **a.** in.³　**b.** in.³　**c.** ft.³　**d.** ft.³　**e.** ft.³　**f.** in.³
2. **a.** 32 units³　**b.** 45 units³　**c.** 35 units³
　d. 343 units³　**e.** 216 units³　**f.** 125 units³
3. **a.** 64 in.³　**b.** 126 in.³　**c.** 16 in.³
　d. 16 in.³　**e.** 2 in.³　**f.** 15 in.³
4. **a.** 6 units³　**b.** 18 units³　**c.** 12 units³
5. **a.** 480 in.³　**b.** 100 in.³　**c.** 700 in.³
6. Answers will vary.
　Length = 2 ft., Width = 2 ft., Height = 6 ft.
　Length, Width, Height = any arrangement of:
　3 ft., 2 ft., 4 ft.　　12 ft., 1 ft., 2 ft.
　8 ft., 3 ft., 1 ft.　　6 ft., 1 ft., 4 ft.
　24 ft., 1 ft., 1 ft.

Page 110
1. **a.** 9 cm³　**b.** 14 cm³　**c.** 32 cm³　**d.** 46 cm³
2. **a.** 2, 2, 3, 12　**b.** 4, 2, 1, 8　**c.** 4, 3, 6, 72　**d.** 5, 2, 4, 40
3. **a.** 80 cm³　**b.** 84 cm³　**c.** 450 cm³
　d. 84 cm³　**e.** 80 cm³　**f.** 128 cm³
4. **a.** 24 cm³　**b.** 2 cm³　**c.** 12 cm³
　d. 8 cm³　**e.** 48 cm³　**f.** 105 cm³
5. Answers will vary.
6. Drawings will vary. Possible labels:
　5 cm x 2 cm x 1 cm　　　10 cm x 1 cm x 1 cm

Page 111
1. **a.** 6　**b.** 1　**c.** 4　**d.** 3　**e.** 2　**f.** 5
2. **a.** yes　**b.** no　**c.** no　**d.** yes　**e.** yes　**f.** yes
3. **a.** 1　**b.** 0　**c.** 0.5　**d.** 1　**e.** 0.5　**f.** 0.25
4. **a.** $\frac{2}{8} = \frac{1}{4}$　**b.** $\frac{4}{8} = \frac{1}{2}$　**c.** $\frac{1}{8}$　**d.** 0
5. **a.** 0.2　**b.** 0.3　**c.** 0.1　**d.** 0.2　**e.** 0.4　**f.** 0.4

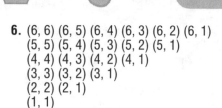

6. (6, 6) (6, 5) (6, 4) (6, 3) (6, 2) (6, 1)
(5, 5) (5, 4) (5, 3) (5, 2) (5, 1)
(4, 4) (4, 3) (4, 2) (4, 1)
(3, 3) (3, 2) (3, 1)
(2, 2) (2, 1)
(1, 1)

Page 112

1. a.26 **b.**24 **c.**10 **d.**6 **e.**16 **f.** 18
2. a.160 **b.**100 **c.**260 **d.**180 **e.**240 **f.** 60
3. a.40 **b.**16 **c.**36 **d.**36 **e.**24 **f.** 16
4. a.60 **b.**40 **c.**40 **d.**90 **e.**80 **f.** 90
5. a.44 **b.**340
6.

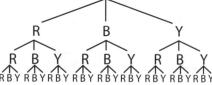

```
          R        B        Y
        ↗ ↑ ↖    ↗ ↑ ↖    ↗ ↑ ↖
        R B Y    R B Y    R B Y
       ↑↑↑↑↑↑↑  ↑↑↑↑↑↑↑  ↑↑↑↑↑↑↑
      RBY RBYRBY RBY RBYRBY RBY RBYRBY
```

Page 113

1. a.–b. Internet, games
c. ⅢⅢⅢ **d.** ⅢⅢ ⅢⅢ
e. ⅢⅢ ⅢⅢ **f.** ⅢⅢ I
2. a.8 **b.**6 **c.**10 **d.**10 **e.**18 **f.** 16
3.

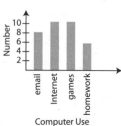

4. a.all **b.**email **c.** Internet and games
d.homework **e.**homework **f.** email and homework
5. a.34 **b.**28
6. a.

```
Ben   ▲▲▲▲▲
Luke  ▲▲▲▲
Sara  ▲▲▲▲◣
Kim   ▲▲▲▲◣
Tom   ▲▲▲▲◣
      Water Balloons
```

b.Answers will vary.

Page 114

1. a.2 cm **b.**6 cm **c.**2 cm **d.**5 cm **e.**8 cm **f.** 7 cm
2. a.$\frac{2}{15}$ **b.**$\frac{6}{15} = \frac{2}{5}$ **c.**$\frac{5}{15} = \frac{1}{3}$ **d.**$\frac{2}{15}$ **e.**0 **f.** $\frac{4}{15}$
3. a.10 **b.**12 **c.**4 **d.**4 **e.**14 **f.** 8
4.

brown		blonde		black	red

5. a.$\frac{6}{20} = \frac{3}{10}$ **b.**$\frac{14}{20} = \frac{7}{10}$ **c.**$\frac{10}{20} = \frac{1}{2}$
6.

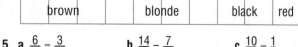

apples		bananas		pears	plums

Page 115

1. a.$\frac{3}{8}$ **b.**25 **c.**$\frac{1}{4}$ **d.**25% **e.**25% **f.** 50
2. a.$\frac{1}{4}$, 25%, 50 **b.**$\frac{1}{4}$, 25%, 50 **c.**$\frac{1}{8}$, 12.5%, 25
d.$\frac{1}{8}$, 12.5%, 25 **e.**$\frac{1}{8}$, 12.5%, 25 **f.** $\frac{1}{8}$, 12.5%, 25
3. a.50 (winter) + 50 (summer) = 100 **b.**same
4. a.250 **b.**200 **c.**50 **d.**300
5. a.$\frac{1}{4} + \frac{3}{8} = \frac{5}{8}$
b.75 (football) + 50 (indoor soccer) + 50 (basketball) +
50 (baseball) + 50 (basketball) + 25 (softball) +
25 (soccer) + 25 (tennis) = 350
6. a.144°
b.90°
c.72°
d.36°
e.18°

Page 116

1. a.60 in. **b.**13 mi. **c.**2,100 ft.
d.28°F **e.**48.5 cm **f.** 625 lb.
2. a.704.3 **b.**2,912.5 **c.**5,662
d.9,554.3 **e.**24,648 **f.** 45,573.3
3. a.70° **b.**75° **c.**65° **d.**70° **e.**80° **f.** 75°
Mean = 72.5°F
4. a.6 **b.**7 **c.**80 **d.**2.9 **e.**250 **f.** 470
5. 73°
6. Answers will vary.

Page 117

1. a.200 mL **b.**300 mL **c.**500 mL
d.$\frac{1}{2}$ **e.**$\frac{1}{5}$ **f.** $\frac{3}{10}$
2. a.$\frac{1}{2}$ **b.**$\frac{1}{4}$ **c.**$\frac{1}{12}$ **d.**$\frac{1}{12}$ **e.**$\frac{1}{12}$ **f.** $\frac{2}{12} = \frac{1}{6}$
3. a.60 **b.**20 **c.**20 **d.**120 **e.**20 **f.** 80
4. a.150 **b.**200 **c.**100 **d.**50 **e.**350 **f.** 150
5. a.$\frac{1}{2}$ **b.**$\frac{3}{4}$ **c.**80 **d.**300
6.

oil	detergent	water	

Page 118

1. a.12 hours **b.**5.5 hours **c.**2 hours
d.10 hours **e.**1 hour **f.** about $4\frac{3}{4}$ hours
2. a.70 miles **b.**210 miles **c.**490 miles
d.350 miles **e.**210 miles **f.** 350 miles

3.

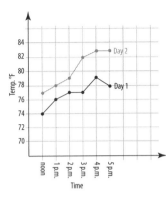

4. a. Day 2 **b.** Day 2 **c.** Day 2 **d.** Day 1 **e.** Day 2 **f.** Day 1
5. a. 1 hour **b.** 280 miles **c.** 5°
6.

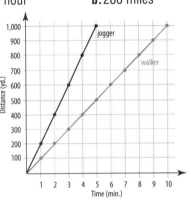

Page 119
1. a. |||| , 5 **b.** |||| | , 6 **c.** || , 2
d. ||| , 3 **e.** |||| | , 6 **f.** |||| , 5
2.

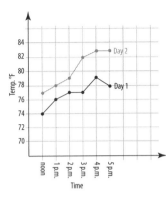

3. a. 13 **b.** 8 **c.** 14
d. rabbit **e.** elephant **f.** koala and badger
4. a. 18 **b.** 9 **c.** 30 **d.** 15 **e.** 19.5 **f.** 16.5
5. a. 35 **b.** 21
6.

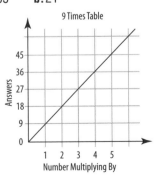

Page 120
1. a. 10 **b.** 2 **c.** 4
d. hazel **e.** brown **f.** brown
2. a. 50°F **b.** 95°F **c.** 32°C **d.** 5°C **e.** 70°F **f.** 80°F
3. a. math and science **b.** music
c. reading **d.** writing
e. reading **f.** math and science
4. a. 65°F **b.** 70°F **c.** 45°F
d. 50°F **e.** Thursday
5. a. 22 **b.** music and art
6. Answers will vary.

Page 121
1. a. 1903 **b.** 1957
c. between 1975 and 1984 **d.** around 1921
e. around 1966 **f.** around 2002
2. a. about 7 million **b.** about 16 million
c. about 17 million **d.** about 18 million
e. about 14 million **f.** about 4 million
3. a. |||| |||| **b.** |||| |||| ||||
c. |||| ||| **d.** |||| |||| |||
e. |||| **f.** |||| |||| ||
4.

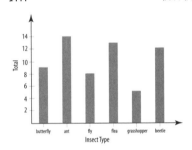

5. a. 1966–1975 **b.** 61 insects **c.** ant
6. Answers will vary. Check charts and graphs for accuracy.

Page 122
1. a. 15 **b.** 83 **c.** 65 **d.** 29 **e.** 447 **f.** 384
2. a. 2 **b.** 3 **c.** 11 **d.** 7 **e.** 12 **f.** 5
3. a. 0 **b.** 4 **c.** 5 **d.** 4 **e.** 8 **f.** 66
4. a. 11 **b.** 12 **c.** 53 **d.** 39 **e.** 1,000 **f.** 40
5. eight
6. 5 boxes

Page 123
1. a. $0.81 each **b.** $0.94 each **c.** lemon tree
d. $12.50 **e.** $0.50 each
2. f. $56.25
3. a. $22.68 **b.** $23.10 **c.** $20.60
d. $23.15 **e.** $21.78 **f.** $26.10
4. a. $2.44 **b.** $13.59 **c.** $5.71
d. $8.46 **e.** $24.50 **f.** $25.33
5. $31.38
6. Word problems will vary.

Page 124
1. a. 11 hats **b.** 86 hats **c.** 37 hats
d. 48 hats **e.** pattern = number of yards + 1
2. d. 125.5 cm
3. e. 770 lb.
4. b. 475 lb.
5. a. 4 hands **b.** 10 hands
c. 18 hands **d.** 28 hands
6. 18 days

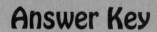

Page 125

1. **a.** 83,105   **b.** 261,969
   c. 1,156,291   **d.** 1,945,769
   e. 5,310,832   **f.** 381,973

2. **a.** 4,713   **b.** 8,431
   c. 3,517   **d.** 7,108
   e. 113,513   **f.** 274,013

3. **a.** 1,215,215   **b.** 532,997
   c. 544,250   **d.** 635,367

4. **a.**
$$\begin{array}{r} 9\,6\,,\underline{6}\,4\,6 \\ -\,3\,\underline{8}\,,5\,2\,1 \\ \hline \underline{5}\,7\,,\underline{7}\,2\,5 \end{array}$$
   b.
$$\begin{array}{r} \underline{4}\,2\,,\underline{6}\,8\,0 \\ -\,1\,9\,,8\,\underline{6}\,3 \\ \hline 2\,\underline{2}\,,8\,1\,\underline{7} \end{array}$$

   c.
$$\begin{array}{r} \underline{1}\,3\,,\underline{5}\,7\,9 \\ -\ \ 6\,,8\,\underline{4}\,9 \\ \hline 6\,,7\,\underline{3}\,0 \end{array}$$
   d.
$$\begin{array}{r} 2\,1\,,\underline{4}\,9\,2 \\ -\,1\,8\,,3\,5\,\underline{6} \\ \hline 3\,,1\,3\,6 \end{array}$$

5. $(1,437 + 1,989) - 2,500 = 926$ oranges

6. $874 total deposits − $755 total withdrawals = $119 increase

Page 126

1. **a.** 8,760   **b.** 27,640
   c. 25,560   **d.** 97,440
   e. 73,450   **f.** 198,960

2. **a.** 71 r25   **b.** 15 r57
   c. 71 r10   **d.** 30 r48
   e. 208 r5   **f.** 36 r29

3. **a.** 1,363   **b.** 1,518
   c. 5,022   **d.** 684
   e. 1,056   **f.** 8,170

4. **a.** 9,495   **b.** 101,307

   c. $5,264 \text{ r4} = 5,264\frac{1}{2}$ **d.** $6,240 \text{ r4} = 6,240\frac{4}{7}$

   e. $4,220 \text{ r4} = 4,220\frac{4}{5}$ **f.** 92,832

5. 10,512 items
6. $479 \times 6 = 2,874$; $2,874 \div 3 = 958$ cookies in each crate

Page 127

1. **a.** 10   **b.** 30   **c.** 20   **d.** 8   **e.** 8   **f.** 7
2. **a.** 8   **b.** 36   **c.** 25   **d.** 24   **e.** 18   **f.** 50

3. **a.** $\frac{11}{10} = 1\frac{1}{10}$

   b. $\frac{3}{9} = \frac{1}{3}$

   c. $\frac{35}{30} = 1\frac{1}{6}$

   d. $\frac{7}{6} = 1\frac{1}{6}$

   e. $\frac{17}{16} = 1\frac{1}{16}$

   f. $\frac{6}{12} = \frac{1}{2}$

4. **a.** $\frac{6}{15} = \frac{2}{5}$ **b.** $\frac{8}{30} = \frac{4}{15}$ **c.** $\frac{5}{42}$
   d. $\frac{15}{32}$ **e.** $\frac{8}{36} = \frac{2}{9}$ **f.** $\frac{2}{14} = \frac{1}{7}$

5. **a.** $\frac{2}{5} + \frac{2}{5} + \frac{2}{5}; \frac{6}{5}; 1\frac{1}{5}$

   b. $\frac{5}{8} + \frac{5}{8} + \frac{5}{8}; \frac{15}{8}; 1\frac{7}{8}$

   c. $\frac{2}{3} + \frac{2}{3}; \frac{4}{3}; 1\frac{1}{3}$

   d. $\frac{7}{10} + \frac{7}{10}; \frac{14}{10}; 1\frac{4}{10} = 1\frac{2}{5}$

   e. $\frac{1}{6} + \frac{1}{6} + \frac{1}{6} + \frac{1}{6} + \frac{1}{6} + \frac{1}{6} + \frac{1}{6} + \frac{1}{6}; \frac{8}{6}; 1\frac{2}{6} = 1\frac{1}{3}$

   f. $\frac{3}{4} + \frac{3}{4} + \frac{3}{4} + \frac{3}{4} + \frac{3}{4} + \frac{3}{4} + \frac{3}{4} + \frac{3}{4} + \frac{3}{4} + \frac{3}{4}; \frac{30}{4}; 7\frac{2}{4} = 7\frac{1}{2}$

6. 4 groups of $\frac{3}{4} = 3$; Drawings will vary.

Page 128

1. **a.** 7.001   **b.** 11.559
   c. 20.915   **d.** 31.733
   e. 41.063   **f.** 58.053

2. **a.** 2.82   **b.** 1.635
   c. 0.533   **d.** 6.079
   e. 4.375   **f.** 0.261

3. **a.** $12.63   **b.** $58.50
   c. $33.28   **d.** $19.96
   e. $22.00   **f.** $13.93

4. **a.** 0.462   **b.** 0.09265
   c. 0.02148   **d.** 0.123245
   e. 4.93   **f.** 0.0046

5. 8.25 seconds

6. $(435 \times \$0.10) + (92 \times \$1) = \$135.50$